# JEREMY IGGERS'
# TWIN CITIES RESTAURANT GUIDE

Copyright © 1991 by Beyond Words Editing & Publishing. All rights reserved. No part of this book may be reproduced in any form without written permission from the publisher.

Printed in the United States of America

ISBN 0-9630942-5-4

Editing: Liz & Steve McConnell
Cover & Title Page Design: Esther Malabel
Page Design: Liz & Steve McConnell
Maps: David Silk
Data entry: Laura Scher, Melanie Moses, LaVette Rainer, Lucia Reif

Thanks to the Star Tribune for permission to reprint material previously published in the newspaper.

Beyond Words Editing & Publishing
P.O. Box 130576
St. Paul, Minnesota
55113-9998

# Contents

| | |
|---|---|
| Introduction | 1 |
| How to use this book | 3 |
| Restaurant reviews | 5 |
| Short orders | 121 |
| Indexes | |
|   By cuisine | 160 |
|   By price | 167 |
|   Jeremy's favorites | 170 |
|   Sunday brunch | 171 |
|   Rooms with a view | 171 |
|   Outdoor dining | 172 |
|   Good with kids | 172 |
|   Late-night dining | 173 |
|   Romantic dining | 173 |
|   By location | 174 |
|   Twin Cities maps | 178 |
|   Alphabetical index | 180 |

# Introduction

What this town needs is more picky eaters.

When people meet me for the first time, they often tell me how much they would like to have my job. I'll admit that it beats digging ditches or cleaning pig barns, but it isn't all warm shrimp flans and gateaux Marjolaine either. In fact, my motto (stolen from a TV critic) is, "I eat out so you don't have to."

It is fun, but it isn't as easy as it looks. And it isn't nearly as glamorous as it's made out to be. While my dinner companions are happily chatting away, I have to spend my evening making mental notes (and running off to the bathroom to make paper notes). And although I do get to eat some very good food from time to time, when it comes to cuisine, Minneapolis isn't exactly Paris.

That's why we need more critics, or at least more critical palates.

Back when I started reviewing restaurants in the Twin Cities about 15 years ago, it was a pretty easy job. If you could tell when food was burnt, frozen or oversalted, you had the basic skills to criticize Minnesota cooking. And if it was none of the above, you had a lot to be grateful for. The local food scene has improved dramatically since then, and we've all gotten a little pickier.

It didn't happen by accident.

Part of the credit belongs to our newest immigrants, who came to the Twin Cities from Ethiopia, China, Vietnam, Algeria, Thailand, France and so many other points on the globe, bringing their rich culinary heritage with them.

And part of the credit belongs to Twin Cities diners, who have been adventuresome enough to try new foods, and demanding enough to force restaurants to change their menus and their attitudes.

In this book I try to give you the flavor of more than 200 local restaurants. Restaurant reviewing is a pretty subjective business, so instead of making pronouncements about which restaurants are the best in the Twin Cities (whatever that means), I've simply indicated which ones are my current favorites. (The list changes all the time.) As you will read, I also like many of the other restaurants listed.

It would be nice, in a way, if restaurant reviewing could be done on an objective basis. I once developed a unit of measurement of food pleasure, called the gastrohedon, that could make all restaurant judgments perfectly objective. One gastrohedon is equivalent to the amount of pleasure in a single ripe red raspberry. (A well-made baba ghanouj, in my book, is worth 10 gastrohedons.)

Using the gastrohedon scale, I would give the highest raw scores for pure pleasure to Goodfellows, D'Amico Cucina and Scott Kee's Tour de France. But considering value, my top gastrohedon-per-dollar scores would go to ethnic places such as To Chau, Caffe Pronto, the Village Wok or the Barbary Fig.

There's just one problem with the whole gastrohedon business: Not everybody likes raspberries.

If you can't be objective, then it's important at least to be open about your prejudices. Here are some of mine: Because I eat out so often, I like food that's novel and creative and different — that's why I like the Dakota Bar & Grill and Lucia's. I am very partial to all of the Oriental cuisines, especially Cantonese, Thai, Vietnamese, Indian and Korean. I do not have a sweet tooth. And I'm a cheapskate at heart, even when I'm spending someone else's money.

Value is as subjective as taste. In most cases, the more you pay the more you get — more decor, more service, more elaborate dishes, more elaborate cuisine. But you don't necessarily get more fun. It often works the other way around. The atmosphere can be so formal that it gets in the way of having an enjoyable evening.

Even with more picky eaters, the Twin Cities will probably never have the culinary culture of California or Manhattan, and maybe that's just as well. Good food doesn't have to be complicated or pretentious. It can be as simple as it is at Peter's Grill, which turns out consistently superb apple pie and vegetable soup.

A good meal in the company of friends can be one of life's great pleasures. If you would like to share your good fortune with the thousands of less fortunate Minnesotans, please consider a donation to the Minnesota Food Bank Network. It's the umbrella organization for food banks and rural distribution sites that supply food to many of the state's 300-plus food shelves. For every dollar the Food Bank Network receives, it can generate approximately $20 of purchased and donated food for those most in need.

If you want to help them with their important work, you can send donations to the Minnesota Food Bank Network, 23 Empire Dr., St. Paul, 55103. And for every copy of this book sold at its cover price, one dollar will be donated to the network.

I've had a lot of fun exploring Twin Cities restaurants, and I hope this book enables you to share some of that pleasure. If you make restaurant discoveries that you think I should know about, please write me, in care of the Star Tribune, 425 Portland Av., Minneapolis, 55488.

Bon appetit!

# How to use this book

Jeremy Iggers' Twin Cities Restaurant Guide is a compendium of reviews, most of which appeared in somewhat different form in the Star Tribune newspaper from 1987 to 1991. Jeremy visited each restaurant anonymously, most of them at least twice. All factual information was rechecked before the book was published.

Although every effort has been made to provide accurate and up-to-date information, please bear in mind that the restaurant scene in the Twin Cities, as elsewhere, changes rapidly. If Jeremy has written about a dish that no longer appears on the menu, understand that some menus change daily, many monthly and most seasonally. Hours may vary by season, too, so call ahead if you plan to eat at an unusual time.

This guide is organized alphabetically by restaurant name. Each restaurant review includes an easy-to-read listing of address, phone number, hours, prices and other details provided by the restaurants, giving you quick access to the information you need to plan your dining excursions. The example at right shows what to look for.

Minnesota law requires that all restaurants provide no-smoking sections. Unless otherwise indicated, all restaurants also reported that they have full wheelchair access. If you have special needs, we suggest you call for details.

**Family Gourmet**
123 Main St.
Minneapolis
555-1212
HOURS
M-F 10-9
Sa 8 a.m.-10 p.m.
Su 10-3
PRICES
$
CREDIT CARDS
AE/MC/V
RESERVATIONS
Recommended
ATMOSPHERE
Informal
ALCOHOL
Full bar
ENTERTAINMENT
Live jazz F,Sa
OTHER
Limited wheelchair access
Valet parking
Sunday buffet brunch

The price categories are based on a typical dinner (when available) at each restaurant, not including beverage and tip:

| | | |
|---|---|---|
| ¢ | Inexpensive | Less than $10 per person |
| $ | Moderate | $10 to $19 per person |
| $$ | Expensive | $20 to $29 per person |
| $$$ | Very expensive | $30 or more per person |

These abbreviations are used to indicate which credit cards a restaurant will accept:

**AE:** American Express
**MC:** Master Card
**V:** Visa
**CB:** Carte Blanche
**DC:** Diner's Club
**D:** Discover

# 4 How to use this book

A review marked with a ☆ means that restaurant is one of Jeremy's favorite places to eat.

The second section of the book, Short Orders, also is arranged alphabetically. These are restaurants that are worth knowing about, whether for one outstanding dish, a unique cuisine or just as a special find. The Short Orders include address, phone number and hours.

At the back of the book you'll find a series of indexes listing the restaurants alphabetically by name, type of cuisine, geographic location and price. There also are special lists of Jeremy's favorite restaurants, as well as restaurants with outdoor dining, attractive views, romantic atmosphere, late-night service, Sunday brunch or a particular flair with children. Finally, we've included maps of the Twin Cities to help you find your way to good food.

# Restaurant reviews

# Acapulco Bar & Grill

The Acapulco Bar & Grill is a Tex-Mex restaurant with a little more variety than most of the fast-food Mexican joints and the chain outlets.

Acapulco's menu is the same as at every other Tex-Mex restaurant in town: enchiladas, tacos and burritos, with a couple of trendier additions such as tacos al carbon and fajitas (beef or chicken). But the quality is reasonably good, the setting is attractive and service is friendly, if sometimes slow.

The queso flameado is a gooey and flavorful cheese melted with chorizo sausage and chopped peppers; very tasty with chips or tortillas. The nachos al carbon with chicken or beef, beans and cheese is a less appetizing appetizer: a big clump of chips glued together with lots of Velveeta-like cheese spread and only occasional clumps of meat and beans. The quesadillas are crisp little tortilla sandwiches, filled with beef or chicken and a melted white cheese.

Best bets from the entrees include the fajitas (grilled strips of beef steak or chicken breast) and the carne asada (chunks of beef sauteed in a smoky and flavorful tomato sauce). The tacos al carbon (soft flour tortillas filled with grilled beef, pork or chicken) actually come pretty close to the tacos sold on the streets in Mexico. The chiles rellenos offer an unusual twist: The egg batter isn't as light and fluffy as it could be, but the stuffing — a mixture of chicken, pecans and raisins — is a treat.

A new "north of the border menu features burgers, turkey and chicken sandwiches.

**Acapulco Bar & Grill**
528 Hennepin Av.
Minneapolis
371-0828

**HOURS**
T-Sa 11:30 a.m.-1 a.m.
Su,M during arena events

**PRICES**
$

**CREDIT CARDS**
AE/MC/V

**RESERVATIONS**
Recommended

**ATMOSPHERE**
Informal

**ALCOHOL**
Full bar

**ENTERTAINMENT**
Mariachis F & Sa, dancing Th-Sa

# Acropol Inn

Acropol Inn
Restaurant
748 Grand Av.
St. Paul
298-0151

HOURS
M-Th 11-9
F-Sa 11-10

PRICES
$

CREDIT CARDS
None

RESERVATIONS
Recommended

ATMOSPHERE
Informal

ALCOHOL
Wine & beer

OTHER
Limited
wheelchair access

I have a theory that all the cuisines of the world can be divided into two basic groups: art food and soul food. Greek food, like that served at the Acropol Inn, is soul food. Art food is subtle and delicate and complicated and takes lots of work to prepare. It developed in countries that had kings or emperors or maharajahs, and lots of cheap labor. Soul food is heartier, simpler and usually made from cheaper ingredients. It's the kind of stuff that can sit on the stove all day while everyone is out in the fields.

The Acropol Inn, owned and operated by Greek natives Aris and Cassandra Apostolou, has opted for a more elegant setting than most taverna-style Greek restaurants, but the kitchen remains true to village style.

The appetizer sampler includes a well-seasoned meatball, a small slice of spanakopita, a stuffed grape leaf, Calamata olives and a couple of slices of a goat-milk feta cheese. The taramosalata (a spread made of carp roe) is ordinarily one of my favorite Greek foods, but the Acropol's version seems to be heavy on mashed potatoes and light on oil.

A combination plate offers standard but satisfying renditions of five traditional Greek dishes: moussaka (layers of eggplant, ground meat, potatoes and bechamel sauce), pastitsio (a Greek version of lasagna), dolmathes (stuffed grape leaves), spinach pie and cheese pie. All are also available individually.

A plate of spit-roasted lamb with cloves of garlic is one of the most flavorful lamb dishes I've had. For more adventuresome souls, squid and octopus dishes are offered.

**Money-saving tip:** Portions are very generous, so unless you have an insatiable appetite or insatiable curiosity, you probably won't need appetizers. You may not have room for dessert, either, though the Acropol offers some fine renditions of traditional Greek fare.

# Afton House Inn

The Afton House Inn dining room has a rustic nautical decor, with gray barnwood walls and old lanterns, and a very continental menu, with table-side service and tuxedoed servers. That may sound like an unlikely combination, but in practice they fit together pretty well. The seafood-stuffed mushroom caps, served with a fresh Hollandaise, have a puffy baked seafood filling that offers a pleasant contrast to the usual greasy mushroom appetizers. Other appetizer options include the escargot, melon and prosciutto, a small order of fettuccine Alfredo and shrimp creole.

The menu offers four light selections, including a larger portion of fettuccine Alfredo, a spinach pasta with smoked salmon, a plate of fresh steamed vegetables with Hollandaise sauce and pasta Alfredo, or grilled halibut with a raspberry vinaigrette.

The rest of the menu offers a wide range of classic fare, from boneless breast of duck flamed at the table to Dover sole, grilled salmon, broiled walleye and chicken cacciatore. All of the dinners include a tossed salad, bread and vegetable.

The offerings on the dessert tray looked storebought, so we opted instead for the bananas Foster, which were prepared flawlessly.

A really picky eater expecting a gastronomic experience would probably be disappointed by the cuisine at the Afton House. But if you approach it with the right expectations, it's a restaurant with considerable charm.

**The Historic Afton House Inn/ Catfish Saloon**
3291 S. St. Croix Trail
Afton
1-436-8883

HOURS
M-Th 5-10
F,Sa 5-11
Su 10-9
(Closed M,T Jan-March)

PRICES
$$

CREDIT CARDS
AE/MC/V/D

RESERVATIONS
Recommended

ATMOSPHERE
Formal

ALCOHOL
Full bar

ENTERTAINMENT
Music F,Sa

OTHER
Sunday buffet brunch
River cruises

# Anthony's Wharf

**Anthony's Wharf**
St. Anthony Main
201 E. Main St.
Minneapolis
378-7058

HOURS
Su-Th 5-10
F,S 5-11

PRICES
$$

CREDIT CARDS
AE/MC/V/D

RESERVATIONS
Recommended

ATMOSPHERE
Informal

ALCOHOL
Full bar

ENTERTAINMENT
Music T,F,Sa
May-Sept.

Anthony's Wharf is one of the few survivors at St. Anthony Main, where countless restaurants and shops have come and gone. While its menu is less interesting than the nearby Newport SeaGrill, the selection of fresh fish plus other traditional meat and chicken dishes can make for an enjoyable meal.

The setting also offers attractive alternatives, including several cozy and private aquarium booths, each with a large tank of tropical fish embedded in the back wall, or patio seating with a nice view.

The seafood platter delivers an ample sampling of crab legs, steamed shrimp, raw oysters and steamed clams. The oysters Rockefeller, prepared with bacon but without anisette, are fresh and tasty, but don't taste much like traditional versions of this classic dish. The deep fried clams don't have much taste of any kind, but are golden brown and nicely crisp and chewy.

The swordfish steak is thick, moist and fresh, served with a commercial-tasting wild rice blend. The filet and shrimp combo offers a very ordinary cut of beef, tender but not especially flavorful, and four large shrimp sauteed with garlic and bread crumbs. A seafood fettuccine contains generous quantities of shrimp with scallops and finely shredded crabmeat in a disappointingly mild cream sauce. The same finely shredded crab also shows up as a stuffing for the fresh and well-prepared rainbow trout, featured as a nightly special.

The dessert choices include a better-than-average cakey cheesecake and a rich carrot cake with too much frosting.

# Austin's Steak House

The steaks they serve at Austin's Steak House are the kind your doctor warned you about: big, fat, oozy, juicy slabs of beef dripping with flavor. One reason they taste so good is that all of the cuts are either USDA Prime or dry-aged.

Eating these steaks reminded me why I find most other restaurant steaks unsatisfying. Demand for leaner beef has resulted in less flavorful meat. I cringed when a friend asked for her rib eye medium-well done, but even this cut was juicy and flavorful.

Beef is the star attraction, but other options include a prime veal chop, tender and juicy prime lamb chops, a 16-ounce pork chop and a charbroiled double chicken breast. Seafood includes a salmon filet, swordfish steak (dry and overcooked), plump and succulent broiled prawns and pan-fried shrimp or snapper.

If you have your heart set on beef but are mindful of its health risks, I recommend the charbroiled sirloin sandwich. The 6- to 7-ounce steak is a sandwich in name only: It's served on toast, but you couldn't pick it up and eat it. It's tasty and fairly tender, easier on your heart and wallet than a big steak.

Appetizers include a cold plate of eight good-sized shrimp with a mild but pleasant tomato-orange mayonnaise, and a carpaccio of paper-thin raw beef topped with crumbled Parmesan, sliced onions and plenty of capers.

You probably won't have room for dessert, but if you do, I recommend the ice cream pie (with layers of Kahlua, coffee and chocolate) and the flourless chocolate torte with coconut sauce.

**Austin's Steak House**
600 Highway 169
Interchange Tower
St. Louis Park
542-8822

**HOURS**
M-F 11-2:30,
5:30-10
Su-Th 5:30-10
F-Sa 5:30-11

**PRICES**
$$

**CREDIT CARDS**
AE/MC/V/D

**RESERVATIONS**
Recommended

**ATMOSPHERE**
Formal

**ALCOHOL**
Full bar

**OTHER**
Limited parking

# Azur

☆

**Azur**
651 Nicollet Av.
Minneapolis
342-2500

**HOURS**
M-F 11:15-2:30,
5:30-10
Sa 5:30-10

**PRICES**
$$$

**CREDIT CARDS**
AE/MC/V/CB/
DC/D

**RESERVATIONS**
Recommended

**ATMOSPHERE**
Informal

**ALCOHOL**
Full bar

**ENTERTAINMENT**
Live music F

**OTHER**
Valet parking

⚜

Azur takes big risks, maybe more risks than any other Twin Cities restaurant. Here your $40 to $50 per person doesn't buy elegance. There are no flowers, no tablecloths, no tuxedoed maitre d's. Instead it buys a fantasy of a different sort: the chance to feel like somebody a lot hipper than you really are in a lively, postmodernly stylish room.

The menu takes similar risks. How many haute cuisine restaurants in this town would feature an appetizer of salt-packed anchovies with tomato bread?

The cuisine is billed as southern French, a rustic and earthy style of cooking. Some of the dishes do seem distinctively Provencal, while others roam farther afield for inspiration: pork braised in Madeira wine with tomato and basmati rice, or sauteed Maine sea scallops with gruyere-parsley raviolini and carrot sauce.

At its best, the food is spectacular. The most memorable dishes include a nightly special of fresh halibut, superbly moist and fresh, in a tarragon beurre blanc served over asparagus and peppery young arugula leaves, and a rich and savory gratin of prawns, field mushrooms and fried artichokes (available only for two or more). There were a few disappointments, but quality overall is very high.

Azur is lively, exciting and uneven. It has a level of energy and creativity that makes many restaurants seem staid and pretentious. If the prices don't scare you off, it's definitely worth a visit.

**Money-saving tip:** Every Friday evening, Azur offers a three-course platter menu (currently $18) featuring southern French, Spanish or Basque cuisine. Diners can choose one, two or three entrees to be served on the platter. A matched selection of wines served in tasting portions is available (at extra cost).

# Barbary Fig

The Barbary Fig gives the Twin Cities area its first North African restaurant. Its cuisine comes from the Maghreb, the thin strip of fertile land along the Mediterranean coast of Africa. Owner-chef Brahim Hadj-Moussa, a native of Annaba, Algeria, does all of the cooking.

It has a family resemblance to the other Mediterranean cuisines such as Spanish, Italian, southern French and Lebanese: ample use of olive oil, tomatoes, peppers, onions, garlic and fresh herbs. Lamb and chicken are common fare, but in accordance with Islamic tradition, pork is shunned. Perhaps the most distinctive characteristic of Algerian and Moroccan cuisine is the staple starch, couscous (steamed cracked wheat, served topped with meat or vegetables in a savory, often spicy sauce).

The Barbary Fig's menu includes three couscous dishes, a tagine (stew) of chicken with zucchini, leeks and tomato jam and several vegetarian dishes, including a tagine of lentils with apricots, walnuts and fresh fennel. The soup, called jary, is delicious: a lively, pungent tomato soup with cracked wheat, herbs and the tang of fresh lemon. The appetizers include a Mediterranean salad and brik (two thin pockets of very crisp pastry stuffed with a seasoned tuna mixture).

The chicken couscous is made of boneless breast of chicken with carrots and zucchini, seasoned with cinnamon and saffron. The lamb couscous is similar, made with chunks of lamb sauteed with caramelized onions, nutmeg and raisins. The vegetarian couscous varies from night to night, depending on the whim of the chef.

For dessert, be sure to try the figs, either fresh (a rare treat in these parts) or dried and stuffed with chopped walnuts or chopped almonds.

---

**Barbary Fig**
720 Grand Av.
St. Paul
290-2085

**HOURS**
M,W,Th, 11:30-2, 5-9
F,Sa 11:30-2, 5-10

**PRICES**
$

**CREDIT CARDS**
MC/V/D

**RESERVATIONS**
None

**ATMOSPHERE**
Informal

**ALCOHOL**
Wine & beer

**OTHER**
No wheelchair access
Small children not encouraged

# Beijing

Beijing Chinese
Cuisine
4773 Hwy. 101
Minnetonka
933-6361
962 Prairie Center
Dr., Eden Prairie
934-3455

HOURS
M-Th 11-10
F,Sa 11-11
Su 12-10

PRICES
$

CREDIT CARDS
AE/MC/V/CB/DC

RESERVATIONS
Recommended

ATMOSPHERE
Informal

ALCOHOL
Full bar

OTHER
Sunday a la carte
brunch

**D**on't be surprised if the menu at the Beijing looks strangely familiar. You may have seen it before — at a variety of other Chinese restaurants around town. My hunch is that it originated in New York and has been adapted by chefs whose limited command of English makes it difficult to produce an original menu.

But while the menu may be the same, nearly every dish we ordered at the Beijing had a different sauce and a different combination of textures and flavors. The pot-stickers were first-rate, though the dipping sauce needed vinegar. Egg rolls were meatier than usual, and the hot and sour soup had a proper balance of spice and bite.

The beef in garlic sauce is thin shreds in a spicy sauce with black tree fungus and sliced water chestnuts. The chicken with walnuts — actually one of the least exciting dishes — is tender cubes of chicken sauteed with diced crisp cubes of bamboo-shoot and crunchy bits of sugar-frosted walnut. By contrast, the sliced leg of lamb Szechuan-style is cut into thin flat slices and sauteed with generous quantities of fresh scallions.

Our waiters were eager to recommend several dishes not on the menu, including general chicken, crisp batter-dipped pieces of chicken in a spicy brown sauce with florets of broccoli; crispy shrimp, deep-fried morsels of shrimp in a light egg batter served with a sweet, light but spicy tomato-based sauce, and tiger pork, very tasty chewy bits of beef stir-fried with fresh, crisp snow peas.

Except for these dishes, there probably isn't much at the Beijing that you can't find at several other places around town. What makes the Beijing worth a visit is how well they do it. This may be the best Szechuan cooking in the Twin Cities. It's also one of the more attractive Chinese restaurants I've seen lately — a modern look with lots of pale wood.

# Black Forest Inn

For my money, this is the best German restaurant in the Twin Cities and one of the best values in any category.

The interior authentically recreates the look and feel of a real German wursthaus, and the menu offers all of the German classics, such as Wiener schnitzel, sauerbraten, bratwurst and spectacular apfel strudel and Black Forest torte, plus daily specials.

There's nothing fancy on the menu (unless you count the Wiener schnitzel), but the quality is consistently very good, the portions generous and the prices very reasonable.

The beer garden behind the bar is my all-time favorite outdoor eating spot. You can choose between open sun or the shade of a vine-covered trellis; either way, it's a relaxing and attractive setting and a good deal more peaceful than its Munich counterparts.

A good selection of draft beers is available by the glass or by the pitcher, including locally brewed Schell's and Summit, as well as German imports from Dortmunder Union, Hacker-Pschorr and Paulaner.

☆

**Black Forest Inn**
1 E. 26th St.
Minneapolis
872-0812

**HOURS**
M-Sa 11 a.m.-1 a.m.
Su 12-12

**PRICES**
$

**CREDIT CARDS**
AE/MC/V/DC/D

**RESERVATIONS**
Recommended

**ATMOSPHERE**
Informal

**ALCOHOL**
Full bar

**OTHER**
Limited wheelchair access

# Blue Point

Blue Point
739 E. Lake St.
Wayzata
475-3636

**HOURS**
M-Th 4-10
F,Sa 4-11

**PRICES**
$$

**CREDIT CARDS**
AE/MC/V/DC

**RESERVATIONS**
Recommended

**ATMOSPHERE**
Informal

**ALCOHOL**
Full bar

**OTHER**
Limited parking

With fish, freshness is everything. From the moment it is caught, fish starts to deteriorate. The Blue Point takes painstaking efforts to obtain and serve the freshest fish possible, and the resulting quality is very high — the best I've had locally.

The cold seafood platter includes plump, very fresh oysters and juicy cherrystone clams, plus firm, large shrimp and half of a small Maine lobster, sweet and cooked just long enough. The hot appetizer offerings include buckets of steamed mussels, steamed clams and crab cakes, made with generous quantities of crabmeat and a minimum of binder.

The fresh fish offerings are listed on a sheet of daily specials. On one visit, half a dozen varieties were listed. Even the thinly cut swordfish is delivered moist and fresh. The same goes for the broiled red snapper and a perfectly done portion of broiled monkfish. These are served very simply, with a wedge of lemon and the choice of a cocktail sauce, tartare or a mustard mayonnaise.

For the true fish lover, this might be all that is necessary. But for my money, an imaginative sauce can do wonders for fish. Without one, I find big pieces of fish a tad boring.

I actually found the Blue Point's nonfish seafood entrees more interesting. The grilled shrimp kebabs offer eight good-sized shrimp broiled on skewers with onion, red pepper, tomato and mushroom, served atop a bed of very spicy rice. The baked lobster is a decent-sized critter, with firm, sweet meat topped with an abundant crab stuffing.

The dessert list is short and sweet: key lime pie, hot fudge sundae, blueberry ice cream and a crisp and nutty pecan pie.

**Money-saving tip:** During summer, the patio menu offers reasonably priced appetizers, soups and a few light entrees.

# Bocce

There's no free popcorn at Bocce, D'Amico +. Partners Butler Square sports bar. Bocce is the latest from the folks who brought us D'Amico Cucina and Azur, two of the Twin Cities' most stylish and trendy restaurants, and popcorn isn't their style.

You can get burgers, ranging from a California burger to one topped with Gorgonzola and pancetta. The rest of the menu runs the gamut from smoky chicken ravioli in hazelnut butter and a lamb sausage pizza with goat cheese and rosemary potatoes to entrees of New York strip, chicken breast with mashed potatoes and grilled pork loin with pasta and beans.

You can't get a pitcher of Bud at Bocce, but they do have some good local beers on draft. A few TVs are scattered around the premises, but they don't seem to be the center of attention. The only sports accents are a billiards table upstairs and a miniature lawn bowling green in the basement.

The food, however, is first-rate. The D'Amicos again draw on their strong suit, Italian cuisine, to offer a menu of intense flavors and imaginative combinations. And the food is given the kind of presentation you might expect at Azur or D'Amico Cucina, rather than Joe Senser's or Champps.

Two grilled slices of pork loin are served with a savory mix of white beans and orchietta pasta, while the tender honey roasted salmon is drizzled with dried currents and surrounded by sliced red baby potatoes and lightly cooked spinach.

**Money-saving tip:** Whatever you order, save room for the spectacular desserts. In fact, if a whole dinner at Bocce costs more than you care to spend, it's worth a trip just for the desserts, including a delicious banana mascarpone cream pie and a great mango shortcake with strawberries and cream.

---

**Bocce**
Butler Square
100 N. 6 St.
Minneapolis
332-1600

**HOURS**
M-Sa 11:30-midnight
Su 10-midnight

**PRICES**
$

**CREDIT CARDS**
AE/MC/V/D

**RESERVATIONS**
Recommended

**ATMOSPHERE**
Informal

**ALCOHOL**
Full bar

**OTHER**
Sunday a la carte brunch

# Brit's Pub

**Brit's Pub & Eating Establishment**
1110 Nicollet Mall
Minneapolis
332-3908

**HOURS**
M-Sa 8 a.m.-12:30 a.m.
Su 8 a.m.-11 p.m.

**PRICES**
$

**CREDIT CARDS**
AE/MC/V/CB/DC

**RESERVATIONS**
None

**ATMOSPHERE**
Very casual

**ALCOHOL**
Full bar

**OTHER**
Limited parking
High tea, M-F 2:30-4

The less time you have actually spent in real English pubs, the more likely you are to be charmed by Brit's. Owner Nigel Chilvers, though British, has made some substantial compromises in adapting the English institution to American tastes. I can't recall ever seeing a pub in England with stools at the bar or a color TV, and the high ceilings, colorfully festooned with flags of the Commonwealth, are more reminiscent of a railway station, or perhaps a hotel lobby, than a London public house.

But authentic or not, Brit's is still a very attractive place to stop in for a pint of ale or cider or a hot toddy. A couple of imported English ales are on tap and the bubbly Woodpecker cider, imported from England and served on draft, is a rare treat. The prime seats are in front of the fireplace, facing the portrait of the Queen Mum.

Brit's menu, like the decor, makes compromises to appeal to local tastes: the fish and chips are authentic English fare, as are the Scotch eggs, bangers and mash, and shepherd's pie. But a ploughman's lunch of bread, cheese and pickled onions, and steak and kidney pie are missing, replaced by hamburgers and steaks.

British cooking has long had a reputation for mediocrity and in this regard the cooking at Brit's is quite authentic. The shepherd's pie is a dull beef stew topped with piped-on mashed potatoes, while the bangers and mash are mealy pan-fried sausages served with mashed potatoes and Brussels sprouts.

The dinner menu includes prime rib, filet mignon and a shrimp curry of the Anglo-Indian variety (with chopped apples and yellow gravy). My inclination would be to stick to the basics, such as the prime rib, the burgers or the fruit and Stilton plate, and enjoy the atmosphere.

Dessert selections include a very nice burnt cream, as well as bread pudding, ice cream and trifle.

# Cafe Brenda

Brenda Langton bills her Cafe Brenda as a "natural restaurant extraordinaire." Although she still emphasizes fresh foods and healthful cooking, she has expanded her seafood offerings in order to attract a wider audience. Unlike many "natural foods" restaurants, the food here really does taste good. Daily specials can include the likes of rock shrimp in a tortilla with chipotle pepper sauce.

The macrobiotic philosophy of cooking emphasizes a balance of yin and yang and makes grains — especially brown rice — the center of the diet along with legumes and fresh vegetables. Strong flavors and rich sauces are usually avoided, as is red meat.

Fortunately, Cafe Brenda's approach to macrobiotic eating isn't very strict. Although the macrobiotic influence can be seen in offerings such as a "sea vegetable of the day" and in desserts made from agar-agar (a seaweed-based gelatin), there is an obvious effort to appeal to a broad range of tastes.

The food is invariably light, fresh, colorful and attractively presented. My favorites tend to be the least macrobiotic: a spicy assortment of dips served as an appetizer, or a portion of grilled tuna, slathered with a very garlicky aioli sauce.

The soba noodle salad, a modest portion of buckwheat noodles, is tossed with a very tasty sesame ginger dressing, and a smoked salmon and trout mousse, served as a dip with fresh veggies, is smooth, rich and savory. A curried lentil couscous soup is so thick, textured and flavorful that it almost seems meaty.

Desserts tend to rely on the natural sweetness of the ingredients rather than sugar. None is of the sinfully rich variety, though fresh strawberries in a pastry shell came close.

**Cafe Brenda**
300 1st Av. N
Minneapolis
342-9230

HOURS
M-F 11:30-2
M-Th-5:30-9:30
F-Sa 5:30-10:30
Closed last week in August

PRICES
$$

CREDIT CARDS
AE/MC/V

RESERVATIONS
Recommended

ATMOSPHERE
Informal

ALCOHOL
Wine & beer

# Cafe di Napoli

**Cafe di Napoli**
816 Hennepin Av.
Minneapolis
333-4949

**HOURS**
M-Sa 11:30-11:30

**PRICES**
¢

**CREDIT CARDS**
AE/V/MC
CB/DC/D

**ATMOSPHERE**
Informal

**ALCOHOL**
Full bar

I have a soft spot in my heart (or maybe it's my head) for the Cafe di Napoli. The Minneapolis landmark dates back to the days before risotto al funghi and sun-dried tomatoes, even before the days of fettuccine carbonara and veal piccata, to a time when (at least in the Midwest) Italian food meant a big plate of spaghetti covered with red sauce. The menu may prompt a wave of nostalgia: spaghetti with your choice of meat balls, sausage, chili mack, mushrooms, turkey, shrimp Creole or Italian sausage; or pizza, ravioli, mostaccioli, lasagna or manicotti.

An awful lot of it seems to taste the same, because nearly everything is covered with the same red Genovese meat sauce. The pasta isn't really al dente but it's not mushy.

I sampled a pizza, a very standard sausage and cheese pie with a thin but not very crisp crust. The antipasto seems rather meager: a few carrot sticks, a few scallions, a few marinated vegetables in a tangy red sauce, a small clump of canned tuna, a few small thin slices of pepperoni, salami and provolone.

A couple of dishes are different. The braccioli are rolled beef birds stuffed with a mixture of bread crumbs, onions and cheese, and topped with a thick sweetish mushroom-wine sauce. The meat is rather thick and chewy but flavorful. The chicken cacciatori is also a better-than-average rendition of this classic: whole pieces of chicken sauteed with tomatoes, green peppers and olives in a rich red sauce. The linguini with white clam sauce contains a generous quantity of chopped clams, but would benefit from fresh garlic and parsley. Desserts included cannoli stuffed with strawberry ice cream, a Sicilian cassata (cake layered with ricotta and candied fruit) and spumoni ice cream.

The dining room has a classic Italian-restaurant mural and a good deal of nostalgic charm, while the adjoining bar is a period piece of late '50s restaurant decor, complete with red Naugahyde-style booths and motel art.

# Caravan Serai

The Caravan Serai has changed and improved over the years since Abdul "Abe" and Carol Kayoum started the restaurant in 1971. The menu has been expanded to include north Indian specialties such as roti (flat bread stuffed with beef or shrimp and vegetables), plus shrimp masala, tandoori chicken and a nice selection of vegetarian entrees, including aushak (leek and chive stuffed dumplings), a vegetarian roti (stuffed with cauliflower, broccoli and carrots) and a vegetarian platter.

One of the most memorable dishes is a simple combination of tandoori naan and hummus, a smooth and rich blend of chickpeas and sesame seed paste. Baking in a tandoori oven gives the naan a subtle but appetizing smoky flavor.

The Caravan Serai serves up a very colorful plate. The most colorful is probably the vegetarian combination, made up of aromatic saffron rice topped with cashews and currants, savory creamed spinach with a homemade farmers cheese, sauteed eggplant in a tomato sauce, thinly sliced sauteed spiced carrots, a mildly seasoned lentil puree and homemade yogurt.

The other dishes I have sampled are less colorful, but no less tasty. The pach e gosfand (lamb shank) is flavorful and so tender that the meat just falls away from the bone; the subzi palow (baked sirloin chunks) are firmer, but not tough. Both are topped with a well-seasoned creamed spinach. I can't sort out all of the spices that I have tasted over the course of an evening, but the more prominent ones include cinnamon, cardamom (I think), cayenne and mint.

Diners can choose between Western-style chairs and tables or seating on cushions at low tables. The decor suggests the interior of an Afghani tribal tent, with billowing folds of cloth overhead and Afghani weaving on the walls.

**Money-saving tip:** A lighter menu on weeknights offers smaller portions at reduced prices.

---

**Caravan Serai**
2175 Ford Pkwy.
St. Paul
690-1935

**HOURS**
M-Th 11-2:30, 5-9:30
F 11-2:30, 5-11
Sa 5-11
Su 5-9:30

**PRICES**
$

**CREDIT CARDS**
AE/MC/V/CB/DC

**RESERVATIONS**
Recommended

**ATMOSPHERE**
Informal

**ALCOHOL**
Wine & beer

**ENTERTAINMENT**
Belly dancing or music T, Th-Sa

# Chez Bananas

**Chez Bananas**
129 N. 4th St.
Minneapolis
340-0032

**HOURS**
M 5-10
T-Th 11:30-10
F 11:30-midnight
Sa 5-midnight
Su 5-9

**PRICES**
$

**CREDIT CARDS**
MC/V/CB/DC/D

**RESERVATIONS**
Recommended

**ATMOSPHERE**
Informal

**ALCOHOL**
Wine & beer

**OTHER**
Small children not encouraged

Think of Chez Bananas as an antidote to gastronomic pretentiousness. At a time when many restaurateurs seem to equate fine dining with eating weird things at outrageous prices in stilted formal surroundings, this little Caribbean-flavored cafe simply refuses to take itself seriously. The playfulness hits you the minute you walk in the door: little rubber bats dangling from the ceiling, inflatable rats mounted on the wall and Etch-A-Sketch toys at the tables.

The modestly priced entrees range from jerk chicken or pork (a Jamaican specialty) to squid Creole or pork medallions with tomatillo salsa. To keep prices down, Chez Bananas offers sensible portions of meat, poultry or fish served with generous quantities of seasoned rice and black beans.

Chez Bananas is not afraid to take chances; combinations can be as odd as a nightly special of shrimp in cream sauce with coconut and bananas or breast of chicken with peanut-avocado vinaigrette. Sometimes, the idea seems better than the execution.

But most of the dishes deliver an imaginative combination of flavorings. The jerk pork is seasoned with slices of fresh serrano or jalapeno peppers and is authoritatively spicy. An appetizer of chicken with Creole sauce is just a notch or two milder — subdued enough for the flavors of celery and olive and onion to come through. The curried pork also falls into this middle range: medallions of pork dry-fried with a medium-strength, green blend of curry spices. Hottest of all is a cayenne sauce that accompanies the Caribbean BBQ tenderloin strips; a mere taste on a spoon was enough to dissuade me from further exploration.

# Chez Colette

The Chez Colette's menu is less adventurous than it was a couple of years ago, but the standard of cuisine is still quite respectable. The menu offers fixed-price, five-course dinners including soup, salad, appetizer, entree and dessert. Compared to a la carte prices, these offer substantial savings, but most diners are likely to find that five courses add up to *un peu de trop* — a bit too much.

Our dinners started with a crusty fresh baguette from the Sofitel's bakery. The soup of the day was a lively, well-seasoned tomato bisque, but our very attentive waiter offered to let us substitute either of the other soups on the menu at no additional charge. The cream of mushroom soup is rich but bland, while the French onion soup is a good rendition of this classic.

All of us were delighted with our appetizers: a generous portion of perfectly steamed asparagus spears served chilled with a mustardy vinaigrette (also available hot with Hollandaise), three fat wedges of cantaloupe wrapped with prosciutto and escargot in wine sauce served in a puff pastry shell.

The entrees are very straightforward: lamb chops with a mint sauce, breast of duckling with a cherry demiglace, very fresh poached salmon with a Nantais butter. My breast of duckling was rare in the center but a little too charred on the outside.

The pastry cart included a delightful fresh fruit tart, an impossibly rich and sweet chocolate concorde of chocolate mousse and chocolate meringue, a chocolate mousse cake, a vanilla mousse tart and fresh strawberries with whipped cream.

**Chez Colette**
Hotel Sofitel
5601 W. 78th St.
Minneapolis
835-1900

**HOURS**
M-Th 6:30-10
F 6:30-10:30
Sa 7-10:30
Su 7-10

**PRICES**
$$

**CREDIT CARDS**
AE/MC/V/CB/DC

**RESERVATIONS**
Recommended

**ATMOSPHERE**
Formal/informal

**ALCOHOL**
Full bar

**ENTERTAINMENT**
Pianist in lounge
M-Sa 5-11 Su 11-2

**OTHER**
Valet parking
Sunday a la carte brunch

# Chez Daniel

**Chez Daniel**
2800 W. 80th St.
Bloomington
888-4447

**HOURS**
M-Th 11-10
F,Sa 11-11
Su 10:30-9

**PRICES**
$$

**CREDIT CARDS**
AE/MC/V/DC

**RESERVATIONS**
Recommended

**ATMOSPHERE**
Informal

**ALCOHOL**
Full bar

**OTHER**
Limited
wheelchair access
Sunday buffet
brunch

Although Chez Daniel's executive chef is Daniel Hubert, one of the area's best-known and most respected cooks, the bistro's food isn't very sophisticated. In fact, it doesn't try to be. This is French cuisine for people who don't like pits in their olives or a lot of garlic in their escargot and who don't like to be served by waiters who are better dressed than they are.

For those diners, Chez Daniel is not without its attractions. For example, the prix fixe five course dinner, offered nightly including salad, appetizer, sorbet, main course and dessert is an excellent value. The escargots I had were a little shy on garlic and the salad long on iceberg lettuce, but the steak au poivre is a tender and flavorful cut of filet mignon, in a pepper sauce that is robust but not overpowering.

Best bets among the appetizers I have sampled are the salmon-wrapped asparagus spears with dill sauce and the mushrooms au gratin, a medley of sliced shiitakes, oyster mushrooms and button mushrooms, lightly sauteed and topped with bread crumbs.

I have had mixed results with the entrees. The bourride Bistro, a seafood stew of monkfish, salmon, shrimp, scallops and crab legs contains generous quantities of seafood, but the the broth is flavorless and the crab legs tasted very old. I did a little better with the roasted duckling with green and black olives. The meat itself is tasty, but the skin is very soft and the accompanying sauce is a much too concentrated demiglace. A companion fared much better with a fresh and flavorful poached filet of salmon in a surprisingly sharp Dijon mustard cream sauce.

Overall, the food at Chez Daniel isn't bad. But what I didn't find on either of my visits is any conspicuous display of talent or imagination.

# Chez Paul

Chez Paul's namesake, chef Paul Laubignat, is gone, and so are the Toulouse-Lautrec posters, but outwardly, little else seems to have changed at this French cafe. The restaurant is split into two sections: the front houses the more casual bistro and bakery, where excellent French pastries are available, as well as cappuccino, espresso and lighter entrees. It's a pleasant place to while away a few hours over coffee; they even provide the newspapers.

Chez Paul bills itself as "affordable, approachable French cuisine," but unless you have deep pockets, you may find the prices on the a la carte dinner menu in the more formal rear dining room a little steep — most entrees are $18-$22. These range from grilled sea scallops on a bed of tomato concasse with garlic, and braised chicken with mussels, scallops, shrimp and mushrooms in a Chardonnay cream sauce, to a steak au poivre with French fries or a roasted filet of lamb in puff pastry. On my most recent (post-Laubignat) visits, I found the cuisine enjoyable, if not especially subtle or creative, and the service uneven; in this price category it faces some very stiff competition.

**Money-saving tip:** The lunch menu (served all day in the bistro) is much more affordable and approachable than the dinner menu. Choices include such classic bistro fare as salade Nicoise, croque Monsieur, onion soup, pate de campagne, a cheese and fruit plate and an assortment of entrees that ranges from lamb sausage with a baked apple and rosemary sauce to a steak with French fries and Bearnaise, all for under $10. The Sunday brunch menu also offers good quality and value.

**Chez Paul**
**1400 Nicollet**
**Minneapolis**
**870-4212**

**HOURS**
Su-Th 11-10
F,S 11-11

**PRICES**
Restaurant $$
Cafe $

**CREDIT CARDS**
MC/V/CB/DC/D

**RESERVATIONS**
Recommended

**ATMOSPHERE**
Formal/informal

**ALCOHOL**
Wine & beer

**OTHER**
Sunday a la carte brunch

# Christos

**Christos Greek Restaurant**
2633 Nicollet Av.
Minneapolis
871-2111

HOURS
M-Th 11-10
F 11-11
Sa 4-11
Su 11-9

PRICES
$

CREDIT CARDS
MC/V

RESERVATIONS
Required

ATMOSPHERE
Informal

ALCOHOL
Wine & beer

Christos offers the most diverse and interesting menu of any Greek or Middle Eastern restaurant in the area. In addition to the usual moussaka, spanakopita and shish kebabs, there is a short list of house specialties of Cypriot origin, including afelia (a stew of savory chunks of pork and potatoes, seasoned with coriander and wine), stifado (a dish of beef and onions baked in a vinegar and wine sauce), keftedakia (a plate of crusty pan-fried meatballs) and sikotaki (a dish of chicken livers sauteed with onions, mushrooms, scallions, peppers and tomatoes).

Other unusual dishes include kreatopita (an appetizer of ground seasoned pork and lamb wrapped in phyllo pastry), shrimp Myconos (sauteed with tomatoes, mushrooms and peppers in a white wine sauce) and a warm appetizer of octopus in a savory red wine sauce. Even some of the most familiar dishes, such as hummus (the traditional Middle Eastern garbanzo bean dip), taramosalata (a spread made from whitefish roe) and melintzanosalata (a popular eggplant puree), seem to have a distinctively different twist.

Desserts include an above-average baklava and several other sweet Greek pastries.

There are a few disappointments: The Bechamel sauce that forms the top layer of both the moussaka (eggplant, ground beef and potato casserole) and pastitsio (ground beef and noodle casserole) is too heavy, and the spinach pie lacks seasonings. And the saganaki (a flaming cheese appetizer) is served with too much Minnesota reserve, resulting in gooey melted cheese.

Those grumbles aside, Christos offers a winning combination: interesting and well-prepared cuisine, a simple but attractive decor and very reasonable prices.

# Ciatti's

Ciatti's offers a stylish setting and very reasonable prices. The food isn't that exciting, but that may not be so important: Sensible people dine out to have a good time and enjoy the company of their friends.

If you aren't looking for memorable food, you can have a great time at Ciatti's for relatively little money. The mainstay of the menu is pasta. I sampled quite a few, including the salsicce spaghetti (tossed with crumbled Italian sausage, mushrooms, onions, and Parmesan) and fettuccine alla Ciatti's, tossed with scallops, bay shrimp, sliced carrots, broccoli and almonds in a cream sauce.

In the past, my big complaint about Ciatti's has been mushy pasta, but of late the texture of the pasta has seemed much improved.

Some nonpasta dishes are tasty, too. The minestrone soup is a rich aromatic broth brimming with chunks of tomato, celery, carrots, beans and other vegetables. And the chicken Marsala is a modest portion of very tasty boneless breast of chicken sauteed with mushrooms in a well-balanced wine sauce.

Desserts are also quite good.

**Ciatti's**
1346 LaSalle Av.
Minneapolis
339-7747

850 Grand Av.
St. Paul
292-9942

14240 Plymouth
Burnsville
892-7555

8010 Eden Rd.
Eden Prairie
944-5181

1611 Larpenteur
Falcon Heights
644-2808

1900 E. Co. Rd. D
Maplewood
770-6691

**HOURS**
Vary by location
**PRICES**
$
**CREDIT CARDS**
AE/MC/V
**RESERVATIONS**
Recommended
**ATMOSPHERE**
Informal
**ALCOHOL**
Full bar
**OTHER**
Limited parking
Sunday a la carte brunch

# Coco Lezzone

**Coco Lezzone**
5410 Wayzata Bvd.
Golden Valley
544-4014

**HOURS**
M 11-10:30
T-Th 11-11
Sa,Su 11-midnight

**PRICES**
$$

**CREDIT CARDS**
AE/MC/V/DC

**RESERVATIONS**
Recommended

**ATMOSPHERE**
Informal

**ALCOHOL**
Full bar

**OTHER**
Valet parking

A strip mall on Highway 12 may be an odd location for an Italian trattoria, but this noisy high energy cafe is true to the spirit and the cuisine of its counterparts in Florence and Milano. The name, which actually means, "the filthy cook," is in fact borrowed from a legendary cafe in Florence.

The pleasure of eating at Coco Lezzone comes in good part simply from the sheer variety of flavors, colors and textures you'll experience in the course of an evening. A good place to start is with the mixed appetizer plate, which offers a generous sampling of half a dozen of the cold tidbits from the deli case. Typical items include roasted red peppers, a cold marinated langostino and squid salad, very flavorful green and black olives, a thin slice of fried eggplant, and frittata (a baked Italian omelet).

Other appetizers include fried calamari, smoked Italian prosciutto with goat-cheese-filled figs, and carpaccio with creamed avocado and hearts of palm. A big selection of pizzas is also available, with toppings that range from asparagus and eggs to shrimp and basil or Italian sausage and gorgonzola.

Different risotto, gnocchi and ravioli specialties are featured daily, as well as an extensive selection of pastas, such as papardelle with grilled radicchio, Italian bacon, mushrooms, tomato and cheeses, or maccheroni with lamb sausage, ricotta and olives.

The short list of entrees includes mostly beef, chicken or shrimp prepared in the grill and basted with flavorful oils and seasonings.

**Money-saving tip:** If you really try to work your way through all of the courses, you'll eat and spend too much. Better to split an appetizer or two, perhaps a pizza or a pasta, and then, if you're still hungry, order cappuccino and dessert.

# Corby's on the Croix

If you turn right when you enter Corby's, you're in a pretty typical small-town Wisconsin bar, complete with TV and video games. Turn left and you are in a surprisingly elegant restaurant, complete with white tablecloths, candles and gilt-framed paintings. The ambience is considerably more elegant than the clientele, which favors shorts and T-shirts.

The menu promises "unique cuisine with a European flair;" the strongest influences are English and French. The pate and cheese plate includes Stilton and Double Gloucester cheeses and Carr's biscuits, along with non-English Brie and chicken liver pate. Other English specialties include Chesterfield chicken, pastry-wrapped chicken Wellington, Cornwall cod topped with crab, rosettes of pork Henry VIII and medieval saddle of rabbit.

Many of these reveal the English fondness for combining sweet and savory. The rosettes of pork mix two generous, very tender slices of pork tenderloin with dried plums and apricots in an apricot brandy sauce; the moist and flavorful rabbit is glazed with honey and cinnamon and garnished with cranberries.

The appetizer of large grilled prawns is tasty, wrapped in tender smoked salmon with a caper vinaigrette dressing. So are the soups, which change daily; I was delighted with a dark and spicy Jamaican winter squash soup and a milder, richer rutabaga vichyssoise. The salad of walleye cheeks (a Wisconsin specialty) with arugula and sweet peppers is a pleasant novelty; the more satisfying starter is a salad of spinach, sliced strawberries, toasted pecans and a Balsamic vinegar dressing.

Dessert options include a sampler of everything in the house; when we opted for that, we got generous portions of a chocolate and vanilla Charlotte, a dense chocolate hazelnut tart, a rich orange poppy-seed cheesecake and a pastry-wrapped pear filled with frangipani.

---

**Corby's on the Croix**
417 2nd. St.
Hudson, Wis.
(800) 657-7010
or (715) 386-1610

HOURS
M-Th 11:30-2, 5-9
F,S 11:30-2, 5-10
Su 12-2, 5-9

PRICES
$$

CREDIT CARDS
AE/MC/V/DC

RESERVATIONS
Recommended

ATMOSPHERE
Formal

ALCOHOL
Full bar

OTHER
Limited parking
Sunday a la carte brunch

# Da Afghan

Da Afghan
929 W. 80 St.
Bloomington
888-5824

**HOURS**
M-Th 11-3, 5-10
F 11-3, 5-11
Sa 5-11

**PRICES**
$

**CREDIT CARDS**
AE/MC/V/D

**RESERVATIONS**
Recommended

**ATMOSPHERE**
Informal

**ALCOHOL**
Wine & beer

**OTHER**
Limited
wheelchair access

Finding Da Afghan in its Bloomington industrial park home is almost as difficult as getting to Afghanistan itself, but it's worth the effort. And while quality varies, if you choose carefully you can dine very well.

Afghani cuisine bears some strong resemblances to other Near Eastern cuisines: kebabs of beef, lamb and chicken are featured prominently along with half a dozen other entrees. The dishes tend to be simple, hearty fare, less complex than Indian, Turkish or Iranian cooking.

Appetizer choices at Da Afghan include pickawra (sliced vegetables deep-fried in a crisp batter and accompanied by a choice of mildly or extremely spicy coriander and tomato-based sauces). It's tasty, but a better bet is the boulanee (flat ravioli-like pockets stuffed with chopped leeks and onions, pan-fried to a golden brown and served with a yogurt mint sauce).

Except for the moist and tender kebabs, most of the meats at Da Afghan tend to be quite well done. That doesn't matter so much in the case of the morgh roast (pieces of roast chicken served with carrot and potato in a savory tomato-based sauce). But a dish of saebzi chalow (beef with spinach) is just about ruined by chunks of meat that were completely dried out and flavorless. There also are several vegetarian dishes available.

The most unusual dish on the menu is the samarook wa rawash chalow (an interesting combination of lamb, mushrooms and rhubarb), which is perhaps an acquired taste. A better bet for most eaters is the kabeli palow (a well-made rice pilaf topped with julienned carrots, raisins and slivered almonds) served with roast chicken rather than beef.

# Dakota Bar & Grill

We have no lack of talented chefs locally, but most of them turn out food that could be found at quality restaurants throughout the United States. The Dakota's chef, Ken Goff, is one of the few who has been successful at defining a local cuisine, in this case based on traditional Midwestern ingredients: tomatoes, sweet corn and peppers, potatoes, peas and great northern beans, pork, beef, rabbit, lamb, quail, chicken, walleye and trout.

Typical dishes can include the Dakota's well-known brie and apple soup, a Scandinavian-inspired chilled fruit and wine soup with sour cream and mint, and broiled fillet of walleye with wild rice, mushrooms and corn relish. None of those is likely to show up on a menu in New York, San Francisco or New Orleans.

Part of what is traditional about Midwestern cooking is its simplicity, and the Dakota is careful not to lose that in making haute cuisine out of humble pie. For example, a thyme-marinated pork loin with maple-blueberry glaze, wild rice and sweet-corn salad and pickled red and golden beets is a delicious and colorful combination that carries just a hint of the potluck church supper. Goff's version of the classic salmon croquettes is made with salmon and walleye and a mustard sauce.

Other offerings have included crisp fritters of smoked chicken and great northern beans, served with a fresh tomato thyme relish and sour cream, or fat and chewy homemade egg noodles, tossed with shreds of smoked rabbit, sliced snap peas and scallions.

Quality of food and service is generally very good. Desserts are excellent, ranging from a chocolate diamond with fresh berries to a whipped chocolate pudding and berry parfait or a generous portion of locally made Sebastian Joe's ice cream.

And to top off a polished culinary performance, the Dakota features an ambitious array of live jazz nightly.

**Dakota Bar & Grill**
Bandana Square
1021 E. Bandana Blvd.
St. Paul
642-1442

**HOURS**
M-Th 5-10:30
F,Sa 5:30-11:30
Su 5:30-9:30

**PRICES**
$$

**CREDIT CARDS**
AE/MC/V/DC/D

**RESERVATIONS**
Recommended

**ATMOSPHERE**
Informal

**ALCOHOL**
Full bar

**ENTERTAINMENT**
Jazz nightly

**OTHER**
Sunday a la carte brunch

# D'Amico Cucina

**D'Amico Cucina**
Butler Square
100 N. 6th St.
Minneapolis
338-2401

**HOURS**
M-Th 5:30-10
F,Sa 5:30-11
Su 5-9
Open at 5
on game nights

**PRICES**
$$$

**CREDIT CARDS**
AE/MC/V/CB

**RESERVATIONS**
Recommended

**ATMOSPHERE**
Formal

**ALCOHOL**
Full bar

**ENTERTAINMENT**
Jazz F,Sa evenings

**OTHER**
Limited
wheelchair access
Valet parking

D' Amico Cucina isn't just the Twin Cities most sophisticated Italian restaurant; it's one of the best restaurants in the Twin Cities, period. It pushes past the territory of tradition to offer a new Italian-inspired repertoire. The pastas, always one of D'Amico's strong suits, range from open-faced ravioli with smoked wild boar, arugula and pistachios, to linguine with zucchini, prosciutto, pistachios and sweet corn sauce. The frequently changed risottos include versions with green onions and saffron or with long-cooked shreds of flavorful duck.

Entree offerings can include a pork tenderloin with smoked pancetta, black walnuts and cinnamon spaghetti, a grilled young chicken with balsamic vinegar, juniper and black pepper glaze, or Atlantic salmon with whole garlic cloves, saffron and mint.

But you may want to concentrate on appetizers and pasta courses and skip the entrees entirely to leave room for the spectacular desserts. Waiters tend to take orders one course at a time, which allows you to gauge your appetite as you go along.

Of the desserts, the crowning glory is the tiramisu, light and delicate hazelnut cake layered with rich mascarpone cheese and topped with cocoa powder. The pear and gorgonzola tart is equally satisfying, while chocolate fans are appeased with a rich chocolate bread pudding in a sweet Chianti sauce.

**Money-saving tip:** On Sunday nights the restaurant features an affordable family menu, including a highly recommended pasta tasting dinner, which includes a soup, antipasto plate and a sampler of two pastas and a risotto.

# Delites of India

Delites of India has gone veggie, culminating a culinary and spiritual odyssey for owners Ameeta and B.K. Arora. They started at a steakhouse in St. Paul, serving vegetarian dishes on weekends, then opened Delites, offering meat and vegetarian Indian dishes. Now they've gone meatless and in the process turned Delites into a much better, more interesting restaurant.

Offerings range from alloo mutter paneer (homemade cheese with potatoes and peas in a mildly seasoned sauce) to baigan masala (eggplant, tomato and potato in a mildly spicy sauce). There also are Middle Eastern dishes, including tabbouleh, hummus and baba ghanouj, and several dishes that roam even farther afield, such as guacamole, burritos and enchiladas. But most dishes are Punjabi — from the area of northern India that borders Pakistan.

If Indian cooking makes you think of curry powder, think again: Nearly every dish seems to be seasoned with its own complex blend of seasonings, ranging from mustard seed and cumin to coriander and asafoetida. There are a few fiery hot vindaloos, but most dishes are mild or medium hot. The complexity shows up not only in entrees and soups, but also in beverages and desserts. Be sure to try the masala chaye tea, boiled with milk and spices, and the lassi (a cold and very refreshing sweet yogurt drink).

The paneer choley is described simply as homemade cheese curried with garbanzo beans, which gives no hint of how complex and savory a stew this is. Same for the tofu korma (a thick scramble of bean curd combined with onions and spices). Entrees include a cabbage salad, aromatic basmati rice and a homemade chutney. In the evening, seven of the entrees also are served as thali plates, with all of the above accompaniments, plus homemade yogurt, lentils, curried potatoes and naan (a whole wheat flat bread).

With advance notice, meals will be prepared according to Ayurvedic principles, based on the season and diner's body type.

☆

Delites of India
1123 W. Lake St.
Minneapolis
823-2866

HOURS
T-Su 11:30-9

PRICES
$

CREDIT CARDS
AE/CB/DC

RESERVATIONS
None

ATMOSPHERE
Very casual

ALCOHOL
Wine & beer

OTHER
Limited wheelchair access
Small children not encouraged
Sunday a la carte brunch

# Dixie's

**Dixies Bar & Smokehouse Grill
695 Grand Av.
St. Paul
222-7345**

**HOURS**
M-Sa 11-midnight
Su 10-2, 2:30-11

**PRICES**
$$

**CREDIT CARDS**
AE/MC/V/
CB/DC/D

**RESERVATIONS**
Recommended

**ATMOSPHERE**
Informal

**ALCOHOL**
Full bar

**OTHER**
Sunday a la carte brunch

The Southern cuisine here isn't very authentic, and that's probably just as well. I grew up in Arkansas and Louisiana and can attest to the fact that, despite the mystique that surrounds Southern cooking, most of it is boring. (Cajun and Creole cooking are a different story.)

At Dixie's, the cooks liven up Southern cuisine by stretching the definition about as far as possible, to cover everything from a Dixie burger (charbroiled over hickory) to Cuban black-bean soup to blackened fish to Southern peanut pepper pork medallions, served in a spicy peanut sauce that resembles Malaysian satay more than anything Southern.

Portion sizes are true to the generous Southern tradition. The barbecue cocktail meatballs, served in a sweet and tangy sauce, are the kind of fodder you can't resist — but then you kick yourself for not saving your appetite. A better bet might be the coconut fried shrimp, four big juicy shrimp in a crisp brown batter.

To their credit, the cooks at Dixie's aren't afraid of the heat. The shrimp Creole soup is spicy-hot and contained generous quantities of small shrimp. The blackened steak also is robustly spicy on the outside and quite juicy and flavorful on the inside.

The one authentic dish you ought to be able to find at a Southern restaurant is pan-fried chicken. Dixie's version is boneless and skinless breast filets, lightly breaded and fried, then drizzled with a honey pecan sauce; quite pleasant, but not the genuine article. The shack sandwich is a better value than most of the entrees — a generous portion of chopped smoked pork on a bun, topped with shredded cabbage and barbecue sauce.

It's a safe bet, though, that a lot of the crowd doesn't come for the cuisine: The main attraction seems to be the big octagonal bar where singles can mingle.

# Dover

At the Dover Restaurant & Bar, the menu is limited, the approach low-key. Most restaurant for hotel guests operate on the motto, "The best surprise is no surprise." They strive for mediocrity and usually achieve it. But the Dover, I was delighted to discover, isn't typical.

The menu covers all of the basics: a few appetizers such as Buffalo wings and chicken cheese nachos, a few sandwiches, such as a grilled chicken clubhouse or a focaccia antipasto sandwich and a handful of entrees ranging from Chicken 269 (a roasted breast of chicken with a sauce of tomatoes, leeks, garlic, olives and butter) to lamb chops (served with polenta and a mint pesto) and a 16-ounce T-bone.

The nightly special when I visited was bowtie pasta tossed with salmon and oyster mushrooms in a rich and savory cream sauce, available as an entree or appetizer (the appetizer proved nearly large enough to be a meal by itself). A cream of tomato soup was also an enjoyable departure from the usual: a pale ivory cream of potato soup laced with chunks of tomato.

Both of the entrees I sampled are recommended: a vegetarian burrito stuffed with julienned carrots, jicama and sliced zucchini, yellow squash and mushrooms, topped with sour cream, guacamole and a salsa of marinated tomatoes, and a terrific shrimp fettuccine, plump and succulent butterflied prawns tossed with heavy cream, julienned peppers, spinach and fresh herbs. My companion and I only had room for one dessert, so we passed up a flourless chocolate cake and strawberry shortcake in favor of an unusual and delicious raisin custard pie.

**Dover Restaurant & Bar**
5555 Wayzata Blvd.
St. Louis Park
542-1060

**HOURS**
M-Sa 6:30-1
Su 6:30-12:30

**PRICES**
$

**CREDIT CARDS**
AE/MC/V/DC/D

**RESERVATIONS**
Recommended

**ATMOSPHERE**
Informal

**ALCOHOL**
Full bar

**ENTERTAINMENT**
Jazz band

**OTHER**
Sunday buffet brunch

# Duggan's Bar & Grill

Duggan's Bar
and Grill
5916 Excelsior
St. Louis Park
922-6025

HOURS
M-Th 11-2:30, 5-10
F 11-2:30, 5-11
Sa 11:30-2:30, 5-11
Su 11-2, 5-9

PRICES
$

CREDIT CARDS
AE/MC/V/DC

RESERVATIONS
Recommended

ATMOSPHERE
Informal

ALCOHOL
Full bar

OTHER
Sunday brunch

Duggan's Bar and Grill does its best to provide imaginative cooking at reasonable prices in a casual suburban setting.

In place of the predictable litany of supper-club appetizers, Duggan's offers such choices as spinach tortellini tossed with artichoke hearts, pecans and Gorgonzola cheese or a seviche of bay scallops and shrimp or steamed mussels served three ways. Entree offerings are just as imaginative, with options ranging from fresh pasta to chicken in a green peppercorn sauce, to a 12-ounce smoked pork chop with red cabbage and new potatoes, plus a variety of daily seafood specials.

Most appetizers are large enough to share. The best among these include the kalbi beef ribs (thinly sliced, broiled short ribs marinated in soy sauce, ginger and sugar) and the steamed mussels (a generous pile of mollusks served with a choice of white wine and shallots or fresh orange and lemon or garlic, cream and basil). The fried artichoke hearts, served with a sharp and tangy mustard sauce, are simple but satisfying.

I've had mixed luck with Duggan's seafood: a mesquite-grilled piece of mahi mahi arrived barely warm, and a serving of Alaskan yellow rockfish almondine was bland. Most successful was the blackened Louisiana catfish.

Red meat may be Duggan's strong suit. The prime rib was a very generous piece of juicy tender meat and a smoked pork chop was thick, lean and juicy. Less impressive were a special of Jamaican chicken (a grilled chicken breast topped with a bland watermelon relish) and a chicken and pasta dish with julienned vegetables in a bland cream sauce.

Desserts, including a delightful bread pudding and a chocolate truffle cake, generally get high marks.

# Emporium of Jazz

I spent several years of my childhood in New Orleans (a nice place to visit, but you wouldn't want to live there), so I have some idea of what real Creole and Cajun cooking is supposed to taste like. At the Emporium of Jazz, some of the flavor of New Orleans gets lost in translation, but enough comes through to make the restaurant worth a visit.

What gets lost, in dishes such as the chicken and andouille sausage gumbo, is some of the complexity that comes from file powder (powdered sassafras leaves) and the mucilaginous texture of okra; what comes through is the spice.

Best bets among the appetizers include the Cajun popcorn crawfish, little nuggets of sweet crawdad tails in a crisp cornmeal breading, served with a spicy remoulade. As the name suggests, they're a tasty snack. The oysters Rockefeller are fresh and good-sized and prepared with the requisite dash of anisette; the Bienville and Casino versions are also up to par.

To their credit, the cooks don't chicken out when it comes to the hot sauce; the pasta with crawfish and the red beans with sausage and rice are both seriously spicy, while the shrimp etouffe is milder but far from bland. The Louisiana plantation platter lets you sample the chicken and andouille sausage jambalaya, red beans with sausage and rice, and black-eyed peas with chicken and ham.

The Emporium also offers a good selection of traditional supper-club fare, including fish, seafood, baked chicken, steaks, prime rib and barbecued ribs. The only dish I sampled from this side of the menu was the batter-fried Gulf shrimp, which are plump and flavorful and prepared in a light, crisp and ungreasy batter.

The Emporium's lounge has another attraction: It features local and national jazz acts.

**Emporium of Jazz**
1351 Sibley
Memorial Hwy.
South St. Paul
452-1830

**HOURS**
M-F 11-11
Sa,Su 11-1

**PRICES**

**CREDIT CARDS**
AE/MC/V/DC

**RESERVATIONS**
Recommended

**ATMOSPHERE**
Informal

**ALCOHOL**
Full bar

**ENTERTAINMENT**
Jazz bands

**OTHER**
Small children not encouraged

# Fair Oaks

**Fair Oaks Hotel & Restuarant**
2335 3rd Av. S.
Minneapolis
871-2000

**HOURS**
Su-Th 7 a.m.-9:30 p.m.
F,Sa 7 a.m.-10:30 p.m.

**PRICES**
¢

**CREDIT CARDS**
AE

**ATMOSPHERE**
Informal

**ALCOHOL**
None

I stopped in to the Fair Oaks Hotel and Restaurant for lunch, sampled some fairly typical north Indian fare and discovered an offer on the bottom of the menu: an Indian feast for 10 or more for $15 a person, with 24 hours' notice.

It turns out the chef is willing to prepare the dinner for as few as five. Our feast started with appetizers of samosas (deep-fried pastries filled with spiced potatoes) and sabji pakora (vegetable fritters). These were followed by long fingers of broiled spiced ground lamb and tender chunks of marinated boneless chicken tikka.

The entrees arrived next: a platter or tandoori chicken marinated in yogurt and spices and cooked in a clay oven, followed by generous quantities of a mixed vegetable curry of tomatoes, peppers, mushrooms and zucchini, a shrimp jalfravy sauteed with tomatoes, onions and peppers and lamb with spinach. Platters of basmati rice and tandoori baked roti and nan breads accompanied the meal.

We washed this all down with sweet, spiced masala tea and tall glasses of lassi, a yogurt drink available either salted or sweetened with honey. Although none of us had room for dessert, we tried a few offerings, which include ice cream topped with mango, rasa malai (sweet cheese curds with pistachio) and kheer (rice pudding with pistachio.) Good food, very good value.

A word of advice: If you want it spicy, be emphatic.

# Far East

Although my anonymous cover was blown early on at the Far East (owners Hoi and So Ching Wong quickly recognized me), I know that the restaurant is at least capable of excellent Szechuan cooking, which is more than can be said for most local eateries that purport to offer it.

The only bad dish I sampled was an appetizer billed as butterfly shrimp, which consists of eight rather small shrimp hidden in enormous amounts of greasy fried batter. You are much better off ordering the fried dumplings (traditional pot stickers stuffed with pork first steamed and then pan-fried to give them an agreeably chewy and crusty surface). The hot and sour soup is one of the few I've had recently that stays true to the concept of this classic dish: It is both hot and sour.

Peking duck is always available. The flavorful meat and crisp ungreasy skin are presented with scallions, hoisin sauce and homemade pancakes.

The secret to Szechuan cooking is a balance of hot, sweet, sour and salty. The dishes I sampled at the Far East weren't overwhelmingly spicy, but they did preserve that balance. Chef Wong has a skillful hand, especially with meats. The combination of a special marinade and stir-frying over high heat gives the meat a buttery tenderness in dishes such as the sliced leg of lamb with scallions or shredded beef with dry red pepper, stir-fried with peanuts and scallions.

Other dishes are a little less spicy, but equally savory, such as the scallops in garlic sauce, stir-fried with water chestnuts, cloud ear mushrooms and green pepper, or the eggplant with garlic sauce, an altogether different dish sauteed with green peppers and mushrooms.

☆

Far East Restaurant
5033 France Av. S.
Minneapolis
922-0725

**HOURS**
M-Th 11-9:30
F,Sa 11-10
Su 4-9:30

**PRICES**
$

**CREDIT CARDS**
None

**ATMOSPHERE**
Very casual

**ALCOHOL**
Wine & beer

**OTHER**
Sunday a la carte brunch

# Figlio

**Figlio**
3001 S. Hennepin
Minneapolis
822-1688

**HOURS**
Su-Th 11:30-1
F,Sa 11:30-2

**PRICES**
$

**CREDIT CARDS**
AE/MC/V

**RESERVATIONS**
Recommended

**ATMOSPHERE**
Informal

**ALCOHOL**
Full bar

**OTHER**
Limited wheelchair access
Limited parking
Sunday a la carte brunch

Figlio — the epitome of Uptown — noisy, stylish, and full of energy. This is one of the most popular bar-restaurants in the Twin Cities, attracting a young, hip, mostly single crowd. Expect a wait, especially on weekends. The best strategy is to wait at the bar — usually very crowded, and watch for your name to show up on the electronic paging board. A limited appetizer menu is available at the bar. Don't go here to propose marriage — your intended won't hear a word you're saying.

The trendy Italian menu covers all of the bases, from designer pizzas baked in a woodburning oven to homemade pastas and tiramisu (the classic dessert of ladyfingers and mascarpone cheese with espresso, rum, and chocolate shavings). This isn't haute cuisine (or alta cucina, for that matter) but the cooking is more than respectable and reasonably priced. Current appetizer offerings include charcoal grilled chicken wings with three-mustard sauce, excellent deep-fried calamari with lemon mayonnaise, and grilled crostini topped with basil pesto, marinated tomatoes and melted mozzarella.

Pasta offerings range from angel hair pasta with spinach, garlic, parsley, Parmigiano, olive oil and pinenuts to ziti tossed with Italian sausage, tomatoes and garlic, while pizza specialties include the classic Margherita (tomato, herbs, goat cheese and olive oil) as well as a pizza Figlio, topped with artichoke hearts, mushrooms, red peppers, onions and fresh egg.

The entree selections include beef, chicken, shrimp, salmon or swordfish grilled over a hardwood fire, accompanied by appropriate sauces or flavored butters, as well as a couple of sauteed chicken breast dishes (with prosciutto and mozzarella or sauteed peppers and artichokes) and a sauteed breaded veal cutlet. Entrees include salad and vegetables. The sandwiches, all served on homemade focaccia buns, are filled with everything from Italian sausage to chicken salad; a selection of hamburgers is also available.

# Fitzgerald's

If you like Duggan's in St. Louis Park and Scully's in Bloomington, you'll probably like Fitzgerald's — all three are owned by the same partnership and feature similar menus. You don't expect a place that looks like a high class coffee shop to have such good and interesting food, but Fitzgeralds has some surprises in store.

The appetizer list runs the gamut from grilled Kalbi beef ribs, Maui style, and steamed Maine mussels to spinach tortellini with Gorgonzola, artichoke bottoms and pesto walnuts, and barbecued sesame pork; the beef ribs and tortellini are especially recommended. In addition to the regular entree offerings, which include pastas, fresh catfish, trout and scrod, and a good selection of steaks, plus prime rib, pork chop, and veal liver, Fizgerald's offers daily fresh pasta specials and a daily fresh sheet of fish from the Atlantic and Pacific.

Best bets from the entrees on the regular menu include the chicken with green peppercorn sauce, the smoked pork chop, and fettucine with chicken and vegetables. The pork chop, hickory smoked by Forsters in Plymouth, is moist with a not-overpowering smokiness and nicely complemented by a saute of apples and red cabbage. The fettucine with chicken and vegetables, tossed with garlic, cream, julienned carrots and broccoli is equally enjoyable — a nice blend of textures and a subtle but lively sauce.

**Money-saving tip:** Fitzgerald's prices are pretty reasonable, but you can save by eating at the bar, where the menu features burgers, sandwiches, salads, soups and a selection of light meals, such as the steamed Maine mussels, spinach tortellini or a stir-fry cashew chicken salad, with a basket of warm rolls, most for under $5.

**Fitzgerald's**
Galtier Plaza
175 E. 5th St.
St. Paul
297-6785

HOURS
Su-Th 11-10
F,Sa 11-11

PRICES
$

CREDIT CARDS
AE/MC/V/CB/D

RESERVATIONS
Recommended

ATMOSPHERE
Formal

ALCOHOL
Full bar

ENTERTAINMENT
Jazz Sa

OTHER
Sunday a la carte brunch

# 510 Restaurant

**The 510 Restaurant**
510 Groveland Av.
Minneapolis
874-6440

**HOURS**
M-Sa 5:30-10

**PRICES**
$$$

**CREDIT CARDS**
AE/MC/V/CB/DC/D

**RESERVATIONS**
Recommended

**ATMOSPHERE**
Formal

**ALCOHOL**
Full bar

**OTHER**
Valet parking

Is the 510 Restaurant the best in the Twin Cities? It all depends. Some people equate the best with the most elegant surroundings and the most elaborate and skillfully prepared cuisine; by that standard, the 510 ranks at or near the top.

The dining room is certainly elegant, and service is impeccable. The menu — a limited list of regular offerings rounded out with nightly specials — is essentially haute cuisine with nouvelle twists. A nightly eight-course tasting menu — which includes an appetizer, soup, fish course, vegetable, sorbet, entree, salad course and dessert — is also offered. The cuisine tends to be more traditional and less innovative than at the other top restaurants, but the quality is consistently excellent.

The food can be sublime and complex — such tasting menu treats as a superb, finely ground veal pate inlaid with dried apricots, raisins and garlic, accompanied by coarse-grained mustard, mayonnaise and chutney. The fish course on one visit was a wonderfully fresh poached salmon in a beurre blanc seasoned with corn and tomatillos. The entree was tender slices of roast tenderloin of lamb atop a fig sauce (flavored with star anise, our waiter said).

Entrees can range from grilled marinated pork loin with cabbage spring rolls and caramelized citrus sauce to rack of lamb with creamed parsley root and chanterelles or a stuffed breast of duck with port wine sauce and pistachios. A couple of fish entrees also are offered every night; one that I sampled, a firm, moist, fresh sea bass in an orange fennel beurre blanc, is one of the best pieces of fish I've had.

The dessert souffles are spectacular; the rest of the desserts are lesser attractions.

**Money-saving tip:** The 510 does offer a couple of options to make dining more affordable: a three-course prix-fix pre-theater menu, and an assortment of moderately priced "light selections."

# Forepaugh's

Forepaugh's serves French cuisine in the setting of a faithfully restored Victorian home. The mood of the place suggests much more the hominess of a bygone era than the elegance of a fancy French restaurant. Service is friendly and not terribly polished.

While the cuisine is French, it also never gets too fancy or nouvelle. The appetizers include a homemade pate of duckling, veal and pork, shrimp with a remoulade sauce (essentially a shrimp cocktail), and escargot in garlic butter. Preparations are mainly classic: shrimp scampi, coquilles St. Jacques with white wine, cream and mushrooms, or veal medallions with calvados and cream. Fresh fish specials and seafood are offered nightly, along with appetizers such as mushroom caps stuffed with shrimp, or a patty of ground lamb wrapped with bacon and accompanied by a curry sauce and chutney.

Although none of the dishes I tried were particularly subtle, all were well-prepared. The *entrecote au poivre vert* was a moist and flavorful cut of sirloin with a lively but not overpowering green peppercorn sauce, and the grilled duckling struck a good balance between a (mostly) crisp skin and moist meat; the honey lime sauce is muted but pleasant. A nightly special offered a tasty combination of sauteed shrimp, scallops, and a well-made crabcake. The ratatouille, a side dish of eggplant, tomatoes, peppers and zucchini, is a highlight.

If you have any room, the dessert cart offers a nice assortment of cheesecakes, English trifle and the like.

**Forepaugh's**
276 S. Exchange
St Paul
224-5606

**HOURS**
Su 10:30-1:30,
5-8:30
M-F 11-2, 5-8:30
Sa 5:30-9:30

**PRICES**
$$

**CREDIT CARDS**
AE/MC/V

**RESERVATIONS**
Recommended

**ATMOSPHERE**
Formal

**ALCOHOL**
Full bar

**OTHER**
Valet parking

# Giorgio's

**Giorgio's**
2451 S. Hennepin
Minneapolis
374-5131

**HOURS**
Su,M 5-10:30
Tu-Th 11:30-2:30,
5-10:30
F,Sa 11:30
-2:30, 5-midnight

**PRICES**
$

**CREDIT CARDS**
None

**RESERVATIONS**
Recommended

**ATMOSPHERE**
Very casual

**ALCOHOL**
Wine & beer

**OTHER**
Limited
wheelchair access

Giorgio's is Giorgio Cherubini's successor to the late and lamented Hosteria Fiorentina. At his old place, Giorgio concentrated on the simple, hearty cuisine of his native Tuscany. At the new place, the fare is even simpler, but the spirit remains.

The main compromise is size. The tiny storefront is roughly the size of my living room. At maximum capacity the place can squeeze in about 30 diners, shoulder to shoulder. There are no tablecloths, the tables are postage-stamp sized and the seating is on backless stools and benches along the walls. As for the decor, there is none to speak of, unless you count the rows of wine bottles lined up against the walls.

The very lack of atmosphere is a big part of its charm: It's a classic "loaf of bread, jug of wine and thou" kind of place. If you go in primed for a wonderful, authentically Italian meal, you'll likely be charmed. If you go in with a little more detachment, the cuisine is still good but occasionally uneven.

Best bets from among the small courses include the savory tart, a pie of mascarpone cheese, onions, olives, tomatoes and raisins in a flaky pastry crust. A casserole of eggplant Parmesan is also delightful. The polenta is served with a different topping every day: on one visit, a rich and savory basil cream sauce; on the next, a sauce of Gorgonzola and sauteed mushrooms. The sauces are very tasty. Four different foccaccia are offered.

Entrees of chicken and roast loin of pork are available every day, as well as a nightly special. A nightly pasta special is also served.

Desserts are simple but well-made: a puddinglike zuppa inglese of chocolate and vanilla custards over ladyfingers, an orange cheesecake made with ricotta, crisp almond biscotti and sweet and crunchy honey walnut torte.

# Good Earth

The Good Earth does not purport to be vegetarian. The menu includes hamburgers, chicken and fish entrees and shrimp, chicken and beef stir-fries. The Good Earth does claim to be a "natural foods" restaurant, but it's not clear what that means, if anything. Although the Good Earth has some of the trappings of a natural-foods restaurant, it has the soul of a Denny's.

The main ingredients that seem to be lacking in the Good Earth's kitchen are soul and imagination. Nothing gives me the feeling that anybody had a personal stake in what this food tastes like. The 12 summer vegetable soup tastes mostly like V8, a far cry from the hearty vegetable soups other natural foods restaurants serve. The nachos, made with tomatoes, onions, jalapenos, guacamole and sour cream are a big pile, held together with melted cheese — filling, but very ordinary.

The walnut and mushroom casserole served over spinach noodles is actually a tasty combination, but a little bit too salty. The fresh vegetable plate is exactly what you would expect — fresh radishes, broccoli and cauliflower florets, celery spears, carrot sticks and the like — with a pleasant dill sauce.

There is far too much mustard on the three mustard chicken and the Cajun chicken breast sandwich is completely perfunctory. I don't know what the "exotic spices" in the planet burger are, their flavor is lost amidst the tomatoes, pickles, lettuce and melted cheese in the sandwich. What remained was the texture, reminiscent of occasionally crunchy refried beans.

One friend complained that his fresh vegetable saute with tofu was undercooked and lacking in flavor; another complained that her Malaysian cashew saute with shrimp was greasy. The dominant flavor of both is soy sauce.

---

The Good Earth
Restaurant
and Bakery
The Galleria
3460 W. 70th St.
Edina
925-1001

1901 W. Hwy. 36
Roseville
636-0956

Calhoun Square
3001 S. Hennepin
Minneapolis
824-8533

HOURS
Vary by location

PRICES
$

CREDIT CARDS
AE/MC/V

RESERVATIONS
None

ATMOSPHERE
Informal

ALCOHOL
Wine & beer

# Goodfellow's

**Goodfellows Restaurant**
The Conservatory
800 Nicollet Mall,
Minneapolis
332-4800

**HOURS**
M-Th 11:30-2:30,
5:30-9
F 11:30-2:30,
5:30-10
Sa 5:30-10

**PRICES**
$$$

**CREDIT CARDS**
AE/MC/V/D

**RESERVATIONS**
Recommended

**ATMOSPHERE**
Informal

**ALCOHOL**
Full bar

**OTHER**
Small children not encouraged

Goodfellow's represents the cutting edge of haute cuisine in the Twin Cities. Arkansas-born chef Tim Anderson, recently named one of America's best young chefs by Food & Wine magazine, specializes in regional American cuisine.

The constantly changing menu can range from carpaccio of Texas black buck antelope with papaya-avocado relish to pecan-breaded rainbow trout with stir-fried vegetables and orange-ginger sauce or smoked pheasant with wild rice-game sausage compote and acorn squash croquettes. The cuisine, while expensive, is consistently excellent — both strikingly attractive and, more important, subtle and richly satisfying in flavor.

It is also original, at least on the local scene. For example, Goodfellow's would never serve oysters Rockefeller. Expect rather something like oysters in an eggplant shell, bathed in a white wine and smoked tomato sauce, or herb-griddled, with a tomato-mushroom compote and pesto aioli.

The entrees are only a shade less imaginative. On one visit, the firm, fresh Gulf snapper was accompanied by blue potato chips and a colorful array of vegetables. The bourbon-glazed pork tenderloin is uncommonly tender and flavorful, accompanied by a raisin and pear chutney and wild rice fritters with a puree of parsnips.

The desserts are ultimate renditions of simple classics: an upside-down pear tart with cardamom ice cream and a warm apple spice cake with caramel sauce, accompanied by homemade pecan ice cream.

**Money-saving tip:** This isn't advertised, but on request, a $10 lunch, including a nonalcoholic beverage, is available in the bar.

# Gustino's

The fun at Gustino's is provided by singing waiters, all professional performers. Their repertoire ranges from Broadway show tunes to Gilbert & Sullivan and Italian opera, and they put on a fine show.

I have found the food uneven and overpriced, but if you order carefully, you can have a good time without spending too much.

My advice is, skip the entrees (which range from chicken breast alla Diavola to seafood cioppino) and instead order either an antipasto, soup or salad, plus an entree-sized portion of pasta.

The antipasto offerings include very small, tasty mussels steamed in cream, white wine and herbs, calamari fritti (deep-fried squid) and prosciutto with melon. The soup selections include a roasted red bell pepper soup and a zuppa di pesce, a satisfying seafood soup full of swordfish, shrimp, scallops and mussels in a tomato stock. The latter turns out to be a smaller version of the cioppino entree.

I had a delightful pasta entree of mushroom-flavored farfalle noodles tossed with roast duck and mushrooms (morels and shiitakes) in a savory cream sauce. Other promising choices include gnocchi (potato dumplings) with bacon, spinach and leeks, spinach linguine with sea scallops, tomatoes and mushrooms in a basil white wine sauce and rotato con formaggi (rolled pasta filled with ham, spinach and ricotta) served over a fresh tomato-basil sauce.

---

**Gustino's**
**Marriott**
**City Center Hotel**
**30 S. 7th St.**
**Minneapolis**
**349-4075**

**HOURS**
M-Th 6-10
F,Sa 6-11 Su 6-9

**PRICES**
$$$

**CREDIT CARDS**
AE/MC/V/
CB/DC/D

**RESERVATIONS**
Recommended

**ATMOSPHERE**
Formal/informal

**ALCOHOL**
Full bar

**OTHER**
Valet parking
Small children not encouraged

# Harbor View Cafe

**Harbor View Cafe**
1st & Main
Pepin, Wis.
(715) 442-3893

**HOURS**
Mid-March to
mid-November
M 11-2:30, 5-8
Th,F 11-2:30, 5-9
Sa 11-2:30, 4:45-9
Su 12-7:30

**PRICES**
$

**CREDIT CARDS**
None

**RESERVATIONS**
None

**ATMOSPHERE**
Very casual

**ALCOHOL**
Full bar

**OTHER**
Limited
wheelchair access

There are a lot of good reasons why you shouldn't jump into your car and go to the Harbor View Cafe. For starters, there must be plenty of restaurants in the Twin Cities area that offer comparably creative cuisine and equal value. I can't think of any at the moment, but I'm sure there must be. Besides which, the Harbor View is far away — 90 miles or so of rural roads — and only open part of the year. There's also the matter of alligators, but there's no point in alarming you.

Have I talked you out of going? Well, at least I tried. The last thing the Harbor View needs, as far as I can tell, is more customers. The restaurant does not take reservations, and the wait for a table on summer weekends can last two hours or more.

The cafe's restored home still has the comfortable feel of a small town tavern. The menu, which changes from week to week, is written on blackboards in the two dining areas. No appetizers are listed, and we understood why when we saw the size of the entrees. A platter of prawns in garlic butter offered ten very large prawns in their shells, served with asparagus over a bed of al dente linguine. The pesce, a seafood stew brimming with all manner of fish in a spicy saffron stock, is spectacular.

The complex Creole gumbo is extremely spicy but also rich with flavors. Desserts are simple but superb — a perfect creme caramel, or a rich white chocolate torte layered with hazelnut ganache.

But simply describing the dishes doesn't quite capture what's special about the Harbor View, where nearly every dish is treated with imagination and given an original interpretation. It all happens at very reasonable prices in relaxing, unpretentious surroundings. So go if you must, but do watch out for the alligators.

The restaurant is entirely non-smoking.

# Harry Singh's Caribbean

Harry Singh's Caribbean Restaurant, for years a fixture in Northeast Minneapolis, has followed its clientele to south Minneapolis. The cuisine here is West Indian (Caribbean), but the East Indian influence is unmistakable. Many Indians have settled in the Caribbean and created dishes that combine their native seasonings with locally available ingredients.

The specialties of the house are rotis (tortillalike wrappers stuffed with your choice of curried beef, chicken, shrimp or potatoes). These can all be ordered in a range of spiciness that runs from mild and average to hot, extra hot and hot-hot, but be forewarned: Even average is very spicy.

The rotis are worth the trip, as are the lentils and the selection of unusual Caribbean cold drinks. Other options include Creole and curried rice dishes, callaloo (made with spinach, okra, coconut juice, chicken and rice) and pelau (a West Indian rice dish made with pigeon peas and rice or chicken). A good selection of vegetarian dishes is offered.

**Harry Singh's Caribbean Restaurant**
611 W. Lake St.
Minneapolis
822-8319

**HOURS**
T-Sa 11:30-10
Su 5-9

**PRICES**
¢

**CREDIT CARDS**
AE/MC/V/CB/DC/D

**RESERVATIONS**
Recommended

**ATMOSPHERE**
Informal

**ALCOHOL**
None

# Heartthrob Cafe

**Heartthrob Cafe**
30 E. 7th St.
St. Paul
224-2783

**HOURS**
M-Th 11:30-11
F,Sa 11:30-12
Su 12-10

**PRICES**
$

**CREDIT CARDS**
AE/MC/V/CB/DC

**RESERVATIONS**
None

**ATMOSPHERE**
Very casual

**ALCOHOL**
Full bar

**OTHER**
Limited
wheelchair access

The Heartthrob isn't so much a replica of a '50s or '60s diner as a tribute to the era — or maybe a parody of it. The menu has all kinds of cutesy names, like the Bobby Ryedeli Sandwiches, I Want My Baby Back Ribs, and Veggie Dip Da Dip Da Dip. Rock and roll pours out from the sound system and some of the waitresses cruise around on roller skates. It isn't quite authentic, but it really doesn't matter; most of the diners appear to be in their early 20s or even late teens, too young to remember the real thing. And they appear to be having a good time.

Classic diner food is simple stuff — burgers, fries, barbecued ribs and chicken. And if this is the kind of food you like, I think you'll like the way the Heartthrob does it. The burgers are big and ungreasy, and the ribs and chicken are moist, tender and nicely seasoned. I had a perfectly satisfactory New York strip steak and a better-than-average Philly cheesesteak, made with generous quantities of thin sliced real beef.

There are a few items on the menu that don't quite fit into the era — the Southwestern grilled chicken salad, served with roasted red peppers atop a huge mound of greens, is definitely '80s fare, as is the tasty lime-marinated charbroiled breast of chicken. And some of the classics are given a new twist. The French fries are given a light dusting of flour, Parmesan and garlic powder before frying, a fine idea. The Bananarama Split has all the ingredients of a banana split, but it's stacked vertically and served in a goblet (not such a fine idea).

The Funky Chicken Wings are served cold with a mustard sauce and taste like Col. Sanders after a night in the fridge. The corn chips are a better bet; they're available with a lively salsa, spicy bean dip and a creamy well-made guacamole.

# Ichiban

This is a Japanese restaurant with stereotypical Japanese decor for people who don't really like Japanese food. The featured attraction is teppanyaki, a style of cooking where diners sit around three sides of a table and watch the cook prepare the foods on the hot grill in the center. Invented in America by Japanese immigrant Rocky Aoki, teppanyaki gives a slight foreign flavor (soy sauce, to be specific) to the kinds of foods Americans are familiar with: beef, chicken, shrimp, scallops and lobster.

Because the food all winds up tasting pretty much the same (like soy sauce), what distinguishes good teppanyaki from bad is the chef's showmanship. The chefs at Aoki's Benihana restaurants are famous for their juggling acts with knives and salt shakers, and the deft way they can flip a piece of shrimp onto a plate with the flick of the wrist. The performance I saw when I tried the teppanyaki at Ichiban showed little skill and less enthusiasm.

Most teppanyaki restaurants I've visited start with a shrimp appetizer; Ichiban substitutes a chicken liver appetizer, which many diners won't choose, and then offers the option of substituting, at half price, from the appetizer menu. (The gyoza dumplings are quite good, but it still felt like a shakedown.)

Ichiban also has a sushi bar ringed by a tabletop moat; little barges topped with plates of sushi float by and you help yourself. The selection is very limited, but when I visited, the fish was quite fresh.

**Money-saving tip:** If you do go, Ichiban has an early bird special for diners who are seated before 6 p.m. The sushi is sometimes featured as a happy hour special at reduced prices.

---

Ichiban
1333 Nicollet Mall
Minneapolis
339-0540

HOURS
Su-Th 4:30-10
F,Sa 4:30-10:30

PRICES

CREDIT CARDS
AE/MC/V/DC/D

RESERVATIONS
Recommended

ATMOSPHERE
Formal

OTHER
Limited parking

ALCOHOL
Full bar

## Jacob's 101

Jacob's 101
Lounge and
Restaurant
101 Broadway NE.
Minneapolis
379-2508

HOURS
M-Th 7 a.m.-
10 p.m.
F,Sa 7 a.m.-11 p.m.
Su 7 a.m.-2 p.m.

PRICES
$

CREDIT CARDS
AE/MC/V

RESERVATIONS
Recommended

ATMOSPHERE
Informal

ALCOHOL
Full bar

OTHER
Sunday a la carte
brunch

Jacob's, an institution in Northeast Minneapolis, combines American and Lebanese favorites at a restaurant with a friendly neighborhood feel. It has a very casual bar that serves budget-priced nightly specials and a fancier dining room with copper-foil wallpaper, bronze statuary and dried foliage that seems to date back to the mid-'70s.

The appetizer platter for two is a Lazy Susan loaded up with nearly enough goodies to make an entire meal for two. A center bowl is filled with homemade pickled radishes, homemade feta cheese and ripe olives; the surrounding trays are filled with hummus (mashed chickpea dip), kibby nyee (raw ground lamb mixed with cracked wheat and spices) and baba ghanouj (eggplant dip).

We kept to the Lebanese side of the menu, with generally satisfactory results. The Sheik's Selection offers another generous portion of kibby nyee, along with baked kibby, a much more strongly seasoned blend of ground lamb, cracked wheat and pine nuts; a stuffed zucchini, stuffed cabbage and stuffed grape leaf, served with pita bread and rather dry popovers.

The loubia (a simple dish of green beans and lamb in a tomato sauce) is made with fresh beans and has a satisfying simplicity. The one big disappointment is the shashlik (a skewer of broiled chunks of beef with onions). There is no sign that the meat has been marinated or seasoned and since it starts out very lean, it ends up very dry.

Midway through our dinner, the owner stopped by to ask us how we were doing. Seeing that I had not put enough oil on my kibby nyee, he decanted a healthy quantity onto the lamb, worked it into the meat with a fork, scooped a mouthful into a piece of pita bread and offered it to me — a very nice, very personal touch.

# Jax Cafe

Jax Cafe dates back to the era when Minneapolis' finest restaurants had names like Charlie's Cafe and Harry's Cafe and sirloin was king of the table. Today, there are a handful of restaurants in the Twin Cities that have the status of local institutions: Murray's in Minneapolis, the Lexington in St. Paul and Jax.

In a solid working class neighborhood, Jax remains true to its traditions: You still get personalized gold-embossed matchbooks when you reserve a table in advance. The dining room has the classic elegance of a bygone era with dark wood paneling and red velvet curtains, pink tablecloths and candle lanterns at every table. But the menu has been updated to include more fish, seafood and poultry.

The kitchen attempts to offer some of that gourmet cuisine they serve downtown, dishes like champagne basil chicken, or trout Veronique, or pasta with shrimp in pesto. But that fancy stuff really isn't Jax' strong suit, or what the customers come in for. The real attractions are the big steaks, prime ribs and barbecued back loin pork ribs, plus the fresh rainbow trout (March through November) from the handsomely landscaped artifical stream behind the outdoor patio. You can even net your own.

Jax Cafe
1928 University Av. NE.
Minneapolis
789-7297

HOURS
M-Th 11-9:30
F,Sa 11-11
Su 10-3

PRICES
$$

CREDIT CARDS
AE/MC/V/DC/D

RESERVATIONS
Recommended

ATMOSPHERE
Informal

ALCOHOL
Full bar

ENTERTAINMENT
Pianist Th-Su

OTHER
Sunday buffet brunch

# J.D. Hoyt's

**J.D. Hoyt's**
301 N. Washington
Minneapolis
338-1560

**HOURS**
M-F 7-3, 5-11
Sa 7-3, 5-11:30
Su 4:30-10:30

**PRICES**
$$

**CREDIT CARDS**
AE/MC/V/
CB/DC/D

**RESERVATIONS**
Recommended

**ATMOSPHERE**
Formal/informal

**ALCOHOL**
Full bar

**OTHER**
Sunday a la carte
brunch

J.D. Hoyt's doesn't look like the kind of place where you'd expect to find steak dinners in the $20 to $30 range. It's a not-very-fancy warehouse district bar, complete with plastic tablecloths, vinyl booths and multiple TVs tuned to sports. But before you go into sticker shock, please note that portions are enormous and that there are less expensive options, including gumbo, steak, chicken, fish or Caesar salad, and a selection of sandwich platters, mostly under $10.

Dinners include Marylou and Wanda's relish tray (olives, carrots, celery, potato salad, pasta salad, herring and fresh fruit), plus garlic toast and your choice of potato. House specialties include hickory-grilled steaks and prime rib, as well as Cajun pork chops, barbecued pork ribs and chicken breasts and assorted grilled fish and shrimp dinners, seasoned with Cajun or Jamaican spices.

Not on the menu, but worth a try, is the buddy bowl for two, an enormous portion of Cajun shrimp and catfish served over spicy red beans and rice.

⚜

# Jenning's Red Coach Inn

Jennings' Red Coach Inn is a throwback to what dining used to be. You get your piece of meat (or fish or chicken), your tossed salad — with the dressing in a little plastic cup — and your foil-wrapped baked potato.

This isn't the kind of restaurant where people go to titillate their taste buds with great cooking, because there is precious little cooking involved. Three basic seasonings are employed: salt, pepper in moderation, and paprika, more for color than flavor. But the Red Coach Inn does offer a comfortable atmosphere, reasonable prices, generous portions and friendly and accommodating service. The clientele seems to be mostly 50 and older: people who grew up with this food and feel at home with it.

The appetizers are basic — chicken fingers, shrimp cocktail, pickled herring with plastic-wrapped crackers — but they're tasty, especially the deep-fried cauliflower florets. The enjoyable chicken-rice soup was obviously homemade and brimming with diced carrots and celery.

The entrees offer a big selection of Midwestern favorites, ranging from calf liver to steaks, lamb chops and a variety of fresh fish. A couple of combinations also are offered: pan-fried chicken with barbecued ribs, or a tenderloin with three large, tender, broiled shrimp. The barbecued ribs, basted with a mild tomato-based sauce, are ordinary, but the crisp pan-fried chicken is tasty. Steaks range from a very juicy, moist and flavorful ribeye to a tenderloin that was neither very moist nor flavorful. The house version of beef Stroganoff is made with tomato sauce in the gravy, which is novel, but not nearly as delicate or satisfying as the standard version.

Desserts, provided by Claudia's, a popular commercial bakery, are a little sweet for my tooth, but my companions raved about them.

**Jenning's Red Coach Inn**
4630 Excelsior Bvd.
St. Louis Park
927-5401

**HOURS**
M-F 11:30-4, 4:30-10
Sa 11:30-2:30, 4:30-10

**PRICES**
$

**CREDIT CARDS**
AE/MC/V/DC/D

**RESERVATIONS**
Recommended

**ATMOSPHERE**
Formal/informal

**ALCOHOL**
Full bar

**ENTERTAINMENT**
Piano bar F-Sa

# Jien Fung

Jien Fung Restaurant
Waterford Plaza
10100 6th Av. N.
Plymouth
591-6085

HOURS
M-Th 11-10
F,Sa 11-11
Su 12-9

PRICES
$

CREDIT CARDS
AE/MC/V/DC

RESERVATIONS
Recommended

ATMOSPHERE
Informal

ALCOHOL
Wine & beer

OTHER
Sunday buffet brunch

Jien Fung is capable of some very fine Chinese cuisine, but you will probably need a combination of persistence and luck to get it. Owner Jack Ma was formerly a chef at the Village Wok, the Twin Cities' best Cantonese restaurant, and chef Wah Tran previously cooked at the Beijing restaurant in Minnetonka, which specializes in the hot and spicy cuisine of Szechuan.

Unfortunately, it takes more than talented chefs to make a great restaurant — especially a great Chinese restaurant. A demanding, knowledgeable clientele is also important, but in towns such as Plymouth that can be hard to come by. As a result, restaurants such as Jien Fung have to modify their menus to appeal to a wide variety of tastes. A generous selection of American-style chop sueys and chow meins is offered, along with other dishes unknown in China, such as egg foo yung, fried wontons, cabbage-stuffed egg rolls and Kentucky-fried style chicken wings.

Cooking styles are also modified. Even when I specifically requested a Szechuan dish prepared very hot and with little sauce, I got a dish that had been toned down and souped up for American tastes.

Your best bet may be to request the special noodle menu, served on weekends from 11 a.m. to 2:30 p.m., which features the likes of roast duck noodle soup, fish ball soup, beef chow fun, seafood and vegetable noodle and curried squid, all at very reasonable prices.

Jien Fung also offers fresh fish and seafood, and fresh Chinese produce subject to availability, but they don't list these items on the menu, so you have to call ahead or ask. Best of the dishes I sampled included the deep-fried squid, a seafood bean curd soup, clams in black bean sauce, sesame beef, and a dessert of fried bananas, a delicious showpiece not available at most Chinese restaurants (and not on the menu at Jien Fung, but worth asking for).

# Joe Senser's Sports Grill

You don't really go to a sports bar for fine dining; you go for ambiance. The ambiance at Joe Senser's consists of 18 color TVs (not counting the ones in the restrooms), permanently tuned to sporting events. Pink neon and an upbeat soundtrack add to the high-energy feel; electronic letter boards flash sporting news and game odds.

As for the food, it's pretty predictable suburban-strip fare: chicken wings and mozzarella sticks, a wide variety of burgers and sandwiches, a few salads and half a dozen entrees ranging from steak and walleye to shrimp and pasta.

The kitchen aims for average and in general hits the mark. Nothing was actually bad, nothing memorable. A few items hit slightly above average: The spicy Buffalo wings are the genuine article, served with bleu-cheese dressing and celery sticks. The shoestring-style onion rings are crisp and tasty. The carrot cake is agreeably moist. And the chicken noodle soup, though perhaps oversalted, is a hearty, flavorful soup that compares well with a premium-brand canned or frozen product.

The most striking feature of the half-pound cheeseburger is its lofty price. Joe's Porterhouse steak is a 1-pound piece of meat, reasonably tender, otherwise unremarkable. The spaghetti is not Al Dente (Didn't he play tight end for the Lions?) and the red sauce with meatballs is the same as that served in dozens of other places that aren't good Italian restaurants. The walleye falls a little short of average, bland and not quite as delicate in texture as the best. A club sandwich is made with American cheese and processed turkey loaf.

---

Joe Senser's
Sports Grill
& Bar
2350 Cleveland
Roseville
631-1781
4217 W. 80th
Bloomington
835-1191

HOURS
M-Sa 11-1
Su 11-12

PRICES
$

CREDIT CARDS
AE/MC/V/D

ATMOSPHERE
Very casual

ALCOHOL
Full bar

# Jose's American Grill

**Jose's American Grill**
Butler Square
100 N. 6th St.
Minneapolis
333-5665

825 Jefferson Av.
St. Paul
227-6315

857 Sibley
Memorial Hwy.
Lilydale
451-0160

**HOURS**
M-Sa 11-1 a.m.
Su 11-midnight

**PRICES**
$

**CREDIT CARDS**
AE/MC/V/DC/D

**RESERVATIONS**
None

**ATMOSPHERE**
Very casual

**ALCOHOL**
Full bar

**OTHER**
Limited wheelchair access

As the name suggests, Jose's seems to be founded on the assumption that if one trend is good, two trends are better. Both Mexican food and American cuisine (whatever that is) are hot, and Jose's menu offers an eclectic mixture of the two: Mexican potato skins and Italian fries, a Santa Fe chicken sandwich, a Cajun burger, a New York steak and duck burritos.

The menus vary a little from place to place. The Butler Square location offers skillet dinners — little frypans filled with eggs and sausage, beef or swordfish, plus an ample portion of fried potatoes and veggies — while the St. Paul location features an assortment of pizzas.

Many of the same ingredients — especially shredded lettuce, chopped tomatoes and onions — show up in slightly different combinations in many items. The topping on the nachos supreme bears a strong resemblance to the topping on the Mexican pizza, which is not unlike the taco filling. The sauce on the Navajo chicken wings tastes a lot like the sauce on the Jamaican beef.

There isn't much point in beating up on the food at Jose's, because it's doubtful that many customers go there for the cuisine. The items I tried seemed designed to be eaten mindlessly while talking or drinking or otherwise having a good time. But hey, that's OK, because people at Jose's really do have a good time. The St. Paul location even has an indoor volleyball court.

Food portions tend to be generous and prices very reasonable. The food isn't bad, just uninspired. A few of the dishes actually are quite enjoyable, among them the hearty duck soup and the lively, meaty duck burritos. The skillet dinner of swordfish is undistinguished, but it is a reasonable portion for about half the going rate.

# Keefer Court

Keefer Court is the closest thing we have in the Twin Cities to the little hole-in-the-wall noodle shops you'll find in Hong Kong or Toronto.

The main business is the bakery, which turns out an assortment of pastries, both Chinese and Western-style. The Chinese goodies include moon cakes stuffed with bean paste or lotus seed paste, egg custard tarts and steamed and baked buns filled with barbecued pork, curried beef and other fillings.

The menu offers typical Cantonese noodle shop fare. The simplest dishes are the noodle and Hong Kong-style rice plates, such as the beef brisket with Chinese vegetables.

For pasta lovers, there are several choices: thin e-fun noodles with crabmeat and black mushrooms, Singapore rice noodles, fried chow mein noodles with various toppings, beef with broad noodles and many more.

If you insist, you can even get sweet-and-sour pork, chop suey, egg foo young and other Chinese-American fare. Be sure to try one of the soups.

**Keefer Court**
326 Cedar Av.
Minneapolis
340-0937

**HOURS**
W-M 11-6

**PRICES**
¢

**CREDIT CARDS**
None

**RESERVATIONS**
Recommended

**ATMOSPHERE**
Very casual

**ALCOHOL**
None

# Khyber Pass

**Khyber Pass Cafe**
1399 St. Clair Av.
St. Paul
698-5403

HOURS
T-Sa 11-2, 5-9

PRICES
$

CREDIT CARDS
None

ATMOSPHERE
Informal

ALCOHOL
Wine & beer

ENTERTAINMENT
Live music F

OTHER
Limited wheelchair access

The Khyber Pass features the flavorful cuisine of Afghanistan in a simple but attractive setting.

Of the appetizers, my favorite is the aushak (thin won-ton-like dumplings filled with leeks and topped with yogurt, mint and a well-seasoned meat sauce). But the bouranee bamjaun (eggplant cooked until it's very tender, in a tomato-based sauce) is also recommended.

The entrees are simple preparations of well-seasoned meats served with a mound of rice and a garnish of ripe tomatoes and onions seasoned with mint and lime. Best bets among the entrees include the kebab-e murgh (a skewer of moist, tender and flavorful boneless marinated chicken) and the korma-e sabzee (a dish of spinach with chunks of tender, long-cooked lamb in a tomato-flavored sauce).

Other options include the aush (a dish of kidney, garbanzo and mung beans and green peas, served over noodles with a yogurt sauce) available with spicy ground beef or vegetarian.

In any case, leave room for dessert, a choice between better-than-average baklava (heavy on the nuts, light on the syrup) and wonderful firni (a delicate pudding flavored with cardamom, pistachio and rosewater).

# Kincaid's

Kincaid's advertising slogan is (or was) "Behind the times. And proud of it." The menu blurb promises to bring you back to the good old days. Luckily, the food at the incredibly popular Kincaid's is much better than the typical fare in the old days.

Take the appetizers, for example. Nobody ever offered Dungeness crab, or coconut beer shrimp with Cajun marmelade, or barbecued sesame pork.

Or take Kincaid's baked chicken Dijon, a breaded breast of chicken with a garlicky Dijon-mustard sauce (a little dry, but very tasty). French's yellow mustard was all we knew in the old days.

Fresh fish? You've got to be kidding. In the old days, fish came in square chunks, topped with tomato sauce, like Mom used to make. At Kincaids, the fresh and tasty mesquite-grilled fish can range from mahi mahi to silver salmon.

Kincaid's beef is locker-aged for 28 days. The prime rib is very flavorful, though chewy in places, and the T-bone steak is tender and tasty. A friend who ordered the double-loin lamb chop proclaimed it the best he had ever tasted. You can't really go wrong here. The menu promises that the steaks, chops and roasts will be flavorful, or your money back.

Kincaid's also has latched onto the trend toward expanded wine and beer lists and, commendably, has included several fine local producers, as well as some outstanding imports. Both food and drink are served amid dark wood, old prints and high ceilings, creating an atmosphere of modern informality.

**Money-saving tip:** Moderately priced appetizers and light meals are available in the bar.

Kincaid's Steak, Chop & Fish House
8400 Normandale Lake Blvd.
Bloomington
921-2255

HOURS
M-Th 11-10
F,Sa 11-11
Su 10-9

PRICES
$$

CREDIT CARDS
AE/MC/V

RESERVATIONS
Recommended

ATMOSPHERE
Informal

ALCOHOL
Full bar

OTHER
Sunday a la carte brunch

# La Corvina

**La Corvina**
1570 Selby
St. Paul
645-5288

**HOURS**
M-Sa 11-10

**PRICES**
$

**CREDIT CARDS**
None

**RESERVATIONS**
Recommended

**ATMOSPHERE**
Informal

**ALCOHOL**
None

*Corvina* is Spanish for sea bass, a popular fish throughout Latin America. Sea bass shows up on the menu in several versions: as an appetizer of seviche, raw fish "cooked" in a marinade of lemon and lime juice (recommended); and as an entree, served either grilled with a garlic butter sauce; or *al cartucho*, baked in a foil bag with onions, green peppers and a wine sauce.

The Mexican dishes are all pretty standard renditions, but well-prepared and served in generous portions. The nachos plate piled high with tortilla chips, sliced grilled chicken breast, onions, refried beans and sliced jalapeno peppers (just enough to get your attention) and smothered with melted cheese, is offered as an appetizer, but it's practically a meal for two. Also recommended are the enchiladas Suizas (chicken and cheese with a green tomatillo sauce) and the cheese enchiladas (with a mild chile ancho sauce).

If there is a fault in La Corvina's cooking, it is a tendency to play it a little too safe; the green coriander rice that accompanies the Peruvian-style chicken looks exotic, but the flavor is quite mild. The only dish I have sampled that is robustly spicy is the shrimp creole, prepared with abundant quantities of baby shrimp. (For diners who want to turn up the heat, a lively pico de gallo sauce is provided with many of the entrees.)

La Corvina does not serve alcohol, but it offers Mexican fruit-flavored soft drinks, as well as various tropical juices, shakes and nonalcoholic wines and beers.

# Lan Xang

Lan Xang offers Vietnamese and Thai cuisine. The owners are Laotian and Lan Xang means "a thousand elephants" in Lao.

I asked my waitress to recommend a Lao dish and she suggested the Special Pheu, a dish I associate with Vietnam. It turned out to be a very flavorful broth loaded with rice noodles, sliced beef, meatballs and shrimp.

On the next visit, I asked the owners to bring a couple of Lao dishes. They insisted that Lao and Thai cuisine are really the same but they were nonetheless happy to oblige. We got a big bowl of tom yam soup — a sour, mildly spicy broth with shrimp, scallions and lemon grass and lab, a room-temperature dish of chopped beef with onions and hot peppers.

I've since tried a couple of other enjoyable dishes from the Thai portion of the menu: the special pad thai (fried noodles tossed with beef, shrimp, chicken, pork, egg and peanuts) and the beef supreme (green beans stir fried with beef in a spicy sauce).

Good food, good value and worth a visit.

**Lan Xang**
1844 Central Av.
Minneapolis
788-1750

**HOURS**
M-Sa 11-9
Su 4-8

**PRICES**
¢

**CREDIT CARDS**
None

**ATMOSPHERE**
Very casual

**ALCOHOL**
None

# Latour

Latour
Registry Hotel
7901 24th Av. S.
Bloomington
854-2244

HOURS
M-Sa 6-10
Su 10:30-2

PRICES
$$$

CREDIT CARDS
AE/MC/V/CB/DC

RESERVATIONS
Recommended

ATMOSPHERE
Formal

ALCOHOL
Full bar

ENTERTAINMENT
Pianist T-Su

OTHER
Sunday brunch

Latour is another survivor from the era when fine dining meant French cuisine. Although the menu now promises "a unique combination of New American and Continental Cuisine," the style is of service and presentation is definitely Old World. The elegant formal dining room is overseen by a suave and polished maitre d', with just a trace of the obligatory accent, and service is provided by tuxedoed waiters, with all the appropriate folderol.

The cuisine is as much New American as French. The French influence is identifiable in a few dishes, such as the escargot Provencal, French onion soup, Bouillabaisse, and rack of lamb Provencale, but many other dishes are harder to place on a gastronomic map: roasted Gulf shrimp, stuffed with Alaskan crab and wrapped with bacon, or grilled chicken on papaya with a citrus chutney, or lobster ravioli served on a bed of spinach.

The escargot swim in a pool of flavorful sauce, accompanied by flecks of sundried tomato and pearl onions that are a little too firm to spear with a fork. The forest mushroom appetizer is pleasant, but not quite as advertised; the shiitake mushrooms are sliced, not stuffed, and the filling is chopped crab, not shrimp, with tomatoes, peppers and zucchini.

A Caesar salad prepared at tableside is one of the best I've had in recent memory. Another salad, of tomatoes, asparagus and blue cheese, was disappointing; the hard tomato had little flavor.

The rack of lamb Provencale lost much of its breading when it was carved at tableside, leaving chops that were moist and tender but not especially Provencale. The sea scallops with black pepper pasta and a rich lobster sauce were an interesting combination, but the lightly broiled scallops lacked the sweetness of scallops at their freshest.

## Le Cafe Royale

The bloom is off the rose at this once-elegant and still very expensive haute cuisine hotel restaurant. All the trappings of elegance are still in place: the gold foil wall coverings, gilded antique mirrors, and the cascading drapes with braided cords, but there are gaps in the carpeting, watermarks on the crystal, and the Villeroy and Boch china has made too many trips through the dishwasher.

The menu is mostly classic French (no surprise since Sofitel is a French-owned hotel chain): appetizers include homemade smoked salmon, a puff pastry shell filled with escargots and wild mushrooms, and coquilles St. Jacques — sauteed scallops and shrimp in a Nantais butter. Entree offerings range from filet mignon in green peppercorn sauce, roasted rack of lamb, and breast of pheasant with grapes in Champagne sauce to beef Wellington, sauteed Dover sole and a grilled filet of salmon with Bearnaise sauce. Less traditional dishes include walleye poached in vermouth with a saffron sauce, or grilled duck breast marinated in balsamic vinegar. Daily specials also are offered, along with a prix fixe menu that includes soup, appetizer, entree and a selection from the well-stocked dessert and pastry cart.

The dishes I sampled were competently prepared, but lacked the star turns I expect in cuisine of this caliber and price. My companion's entree, a sauteed breast of chicken served over a tasty wild mushroom risotto, sat on a tableside cart cooling off while our server deboned my Dover sole. This procedure, ordinarily an occasion for showmanship, was awkward because the fish had gotten stuck to the bottom of the pan. The sole was quite fresh, but some of the delicacy was lost in the excess of melted butter, which also coated all of the accompanying vegetables.

Le Cafe Royale
Hotel Sofitel
5601 W. 78th St.
Minneapolis
835-1900

HOURS
M-F 11:30-2, 6-10
Sa 6-10

PRICES

CREDIT CARDS
AE/MC/V/CB/DC

RESERVATIONS
Required

ATMOSPHERE
Formal

ALCOHOL
Full bar

OTHER
Small children not encouraged

# Le Carrousel

Le Carrousel
Radisson Hotel
11 E. Kellogg Blvd.
St. Paul
292-1900

HOURS
M-Th 11:30-2,
5:30-10:30
F 11:30-2,
5:30-11:30
Sa 5:30-11:30

PRICES
$$

CREDIT CARDS
AE/MC/V/
CB/DC/D

RESERVATIONS
Recommended

ATMOSPHERE
Formal

ALCOHOL
Full bar

ENTERTAINMENT
Pianist nightly

As with most novelty restaurants, whether Le Carrousel's gimmick — a revolving dining platform with a leisurely and panoramic view of the St. Paul skyline — is worth the price probably depends on what you value most when you dine out. Le Carrousel can serve up a memorable evening, but it does not serve creative cuisine. What it does serve is very respectable "gourmet" hotel cooking: a wide selection of steaks and chops, plus an assortment of seafood and poultry dishes, occasionally with an unusual sauce.

The appetizer selection includes a large but dull baked Brie in phyllo dough with toast rounds, a very modest portion of smoked salmon of very average quality and mushroom caps escargot served on a bed of very savory pesto sauce.

For the most part, the entrees are very straightforward preparations, which means that the final result depends a great deal on the quality of the raw ingredients. I found the prime rib first-rate, but the lamb chops rather chewy and underdone. The shrimp scampi and coconut tempura shrimp are both full of flavor, but the citrus sea scallops, served on a bed of spinach linguine, are a disappointment, with a faintly bitter taste.

All of the other entrees I sampled are winners: a fresh and delicately flavored rainbow trout with a pecan crust, a salmon fillet glazed with brown sugar and baked in parchment and a sauteed breast of pheasant with a mushroom sauce.

Desserts include an assortment of cakes and tortes. The best bet is the flaming bananas Foster prepared at table side with appropriate pyrotechnics.

# Lexington

'My dad used to love this place," a friend said midway through our dinner at the Lexington Restaurant. His comment pointed up the differences between what the four of us (all 30-something) want from a restaurant, and what our parents expect.

We all found the Lexington's food generally pretty good, but not creative or interesting or unusual. But when my friend's father dined out, he wasn't looking for creative, unusual or interesting. He wanted a steak and a baked potato, washed down with a martini and a cup of coffee.

To stay in business, the Lexington must replace customers like my friend's father (who died several years ago) with customers like us. That means walking a delicate line: Change too slowly and you become obsolete, change too quickly and you risk alienating your longtime customers.

The Lexington is cautiously seeking that balance with a gradually changing menu, while retaining the ambience and aura of tradition that make it a very comfortable place to dine. The appetizer list now offers grilled shrimp marinated in lemon soy served over red cabbage and a baked goat cheese fondue (both recommended), but the old favorites are offered as well: a classic shrimp cocktail, very good crisp onion rings and a first-rate chicken-liver paté.

The entree list still gives steaks and chops top billing, but includes such unexpected items as spicy chicken Tchopitoulas, shrimp linguini and chicken broccoli fettuccine, plus fresh fish and seafood specials. The immense steer tenderloin was tender but not exceptionally juicy or flavorful. The chicken Tchopitoulas, a chicken breast with Bearnaise sauce over diced potatoes and ham, is heavily seasoned with fiery Cajun spices; I rather liked it, but many diners are likely to find it too hot.

**Money-saving tip:** The snack menu, served after 8:30 p.m., includes pastas, eggs Benedict and a clubhouse sandwich.

---

**Lexington Restaurant**
1096 Grand Av.
St. Paul
222-5878

HOURS
M-Sa 11-midnight

PRICES
$$

CREDIT CARDS
MC/V/CB/D

RESERVATIONS
Recommended

ATMOSPHERE
Formal

ALCOHOL
Full bar

OTHER
Limited parking
Sunday a la carte brunch

# Living Room

☆

**Living Room**
256 1st Av. N
Minneapolis
343-0360

**HOURS**
M-Th 11-3, 5:30-11
F 11-3, 5:30-2
Sa 5:30-2

**PRICES**
$

**CREDIT CARDS**
AE/MC/V/
CB/DC/D

**RESERVATIONS**
Recommended

**ATMOSPHERE**
Very casual

**ALCOHOL**
Full bar

**OTHER**
Limited parking

The Living Room doesn't actually look that much like a living room. The bar looks more like a spoof of an elegant '40s hotel lounge, complete with fireplace, chandeliers and overstuffed armchairs, while the dining room looks like a loopy tribute to the supper clubs of the same era, complete with gilded mirrors, swooping red velvet drapes and fake old masters on the dark green walls.

Of course, the Living Room isn't really a '40s hotel lounge, or a supper club; it's just playing make-believe. Striking poses. Which seems to be what the '90s are all about. Luckily, the kitchen staff takes its work seriously.

Chef Richard Truax has real talent. In the best '90s style, he borrows freely, putting together menus that change weekly, with pasta and seafood specials that change nightly. His style is a pastiche: norimaki sushi borrowed from the Japanese and empanadita appetizers of South American provenance, side by side with Jamaican jerk chicken and beef medallions in Bourbon mustard sauce. Not every dish is successful, but Truax has a very high batting average.

He also has a knack for combining flavors: A nightly special of fresh grilled yellowfin tuna with a spicy avocado salsa was a successful combination, as was the mating of grilled lamb chops and figs. Sliced loin of roast pork, cooked pink and stuffed with cheese, apples and nuts, over a roasted yellow tomato sauce is a delicate and savory combination, while the Jamaican jerk chicken with ginger and curry is more robust, not really hot, but intensely savory. A nightly pasta special was a delightful combination of black squid ink pasta and a generous quantity of lightly cooked large and sweet white sea scallops with a mild but savory saffron cream sauce.

Overall, the Living Room offers a winning combination — a comfortable setting, reasonable prices, very fine cuisine and attentive service.

# Loring Cafe

If the Loring Cafe is the local Vatican of hipness, then the adjoining Loring Bar is the Sistine Chapel. Heavy on garlic, very heavy on attitude (especially at the Bar), but the saving grace is the cuisine, which is occasionally uneven, but generally imaginative and well-prepared. The Bar offers a limited menu of pastas and salads at very reasonable prices.

If there is a distinctive Twin Cities cuisine, it's captured in bistro-restaurants like the Loring Cafe. It's a California cuisine adapted to northern climes — a little less flamboyant, a little more sensible, flavored by the strong local interest in natural and macrobiotic foods. The Loring's menu offers a handful of appetizers, including a lively warm artichoke spread for two, flavored with green chilis and Parmesan and accompanied by grilled garlic bread, and a baked round of Bucheron goat cheese for two, served in a chunky tomato sauce and accompanied by grilled green pesto bread.

The menu changes frequently. When I last visited, the pasta offerings included pasta marinara and a seafood linguini of shrimp and scallops in a fresh tomato and basil sauce. Salads include a smoked duck salad on spinach and endive with egg, bacon and brown sugar vinaigrette, and a warm shiitake mushroom spinach salad with a sorrel and shallot cream dressing.

Entrees include a ribeye steak with Gorgonzola and cran-raisins, shrimp with pears and green peppercorns, osso bucco in tomato and saffron, and a lamb stew with sun-dried tomatoes and blackeyed peas. A sauteed breast of chicken topped with a well-balanced lemon caper sauce was a winner. Several pizzas are also offered, with toppings of (your choice) Italian sausage and roasted peppers, goat cheese and sun-dried tomatoes, mushrooms, basil and Parmesan, or barbecued chicken.

The outdoor courtyard is one of the most romantic dining spots in the Twin Cities.

---

**The Loring Cafe**
1624 Harmon Pl.
Minneapolis
338-6258

**HOURS**
M-Th 11:30-2:30, 5:30-11
F 11:30-2:30, 5:30-12
Sa 5:30-12
Su 5-10

**PRICES**
$$

**CREDIT CARDS**
MC/V

**RESERVATIONS**
Recommended

**ATMOSPHERE**
Informal

**ALCOHOL**
Wine & beer

**ENTERTAINMENT**
Solo saxophone nightly

**OTHER**
Limited wheelchair access

# Lowell Inn

**Lowell Inn**
102 N. 2nd St.
Stillwater
439-1100

**HOURS**
Daily
8-10, 12-2,
5-9

**PRICES**

**CREDIT CARDS**
MC/V

**RESERVATIONS**
Required

**ATMOSPHERE**
Formal

**ALCOHOL**
Full bar

You're either going to be captivated by the Lowell Inn's two restaurants, or you're not. If you are, you'll go home feeling that you had a unique and charming dining experience. If you can't get with the program, the whole experience is likely to strike you as a little pretentious and quite expensive.

Dinner in the George Washington Room is a trip back in time. The room is filled with antique silver and porcelain and the menu is mostly Americana served by costumed waitresses in period dress. The food is simple traditional fare, but the quality is unimpressive. The fried chicken and breaded shrimp are rather dry and, though the sirloin steak is reasonably tender, it isn't especially flavorful. Among the entrees, only the chicken livers drew a positive reaction. The accompaniments, such as creamed squash, red cabbage and mashed potatoes and gravy, are more satisfying, but the desserts are mediocre.

The Matterhorn Room, elaborately decorated with Swiss woodcarvings and stained glass, specializes in fondue Bourguignon. This is a do-it-yourself dinner in which you dip chunks of raw sirloin or breaded shrimp into a pot of bubbling hot oil. Four different wines are served (included in the fixed price) and the servers are quite diligent about refilling glasses.

The dinner begins with half a dozen snails served in the shell with garlic butter, followed by a salad of iceberg and romaine lettuces with a choice of four dressings. The beef and shrimp fondue is accompanied by a relish tray and includes several dipping sauces: anchovy butter, Bordelaise (mushroom and wine), Bearnaise (butter and tarragon), caper, barbecue and tangy Spanish tomato. Dessert is a pewter cup filled with fresh grapes, topped with brown sugar.

Service is prompt, attentive and unobtrusive. The wine flowed abundantly, the evening flowed smoothly, and I went away full and happy, though a bit bothered by how much of the meal came from a can, jar, or box.

# Lowry's

Lowry's, which started out as a bare bones bistro with a simple menu of pasta, polenta and risotto, has blossomed into a very fine restaurant, without losing its original charm. The menu is basically Italian, but with occasional influences from as far away as Mexico, Greece and the Orient.

Typical dishes include grilled polenta with your choice of ancho pepper, marinara or black bean sauce, fettuccine with eggplant, spinach, garlic, olive oil and Parmesan, scallops with peanut ginger sauce over linguine and nightly specials that range from a chicken breast with a tangerine walnut sauce to a baked meatloaf with roasted pepper-tomato sauce, rice and delicotta squash.

Lowry's offers good quality and very good value. The pastas and the risotto are served al dente and the sauces are usually lively and fresh-tasting.

I had an excellent banana cheesecake on one visit, a very rich and chocolatey cake on another.

Lowry's also serves lunch (a shortened version of the dinner menu), a Sunday a la carte brunch and Saturday breakfast. Cafe au lait and espresso are available and there is a short, reasonably priced wine and beer list.

The ambiance is simple but attractive, service is casual and friendly.

**Lowry's Cafe**
1934 S. Hennepin
Minneapolis
871-0806

HOURS
M-Th 11-10
F 11-11
Sa 10-11
Su 10-10

PRICES
$

CREDIT CARDS
AE/MC/V

RESERVATIONS
Recommended

ATMOSPHERE
Informal

ALCOHOL
Wine & beer

OTHER
Small children not encouraged
Sunday a la carte brunch

# Lucia's

Lucia's Restaurant
1432 W. 31st St.
Minneapolis
825-1572

**HOURS**
T-Th 11:30-2:30,
5:30-9:30
F 11:30-2:30,
5:30-10
Sa 10-2, 5:30-10
Su 10-2, 5:30-9
Closed week of
Uptown Art Fair

**PRICES**
$$

**CREDIT CARDS**
MC/V

**RESERVATIONS**
Recommended

**ATMOSPHERE**
Informal

**ALCOHOL**
Wine & beer

**OTHER**
Limited parking
Sunday a la carte
brunch

Lucia's is one of the finest and purest local examples of a chef's restaurant, where the chef — in this case Lucia Watson — has total artistic control and the cuisine is a very personal expression of the chef's tastes and vision. There is an uncluttered and elegant simplicity to every aspect of the restaurant: the decor, the menu and the cuisine itself.

Watson's dinner menu usually offers four entrees, including a vegetarian entree, a chicken dish, a red meat offering and a fish or seafood selection, while the lunch menu offers half a dozen choices.

The selections change daily, but offerings have included polenta with a sun-dried tomato pesto; chicken breast with a wild mushroom stuffing, braised lamb shank with a rosemary mint aioli, and sauteed scallops with a Bourbon beurre blanc.

The a la carte Sunday brunch menu, which also changes regularly, features such fare as a dilled Havarti cheese omelet with fresh dill and oven-roasted potatoes, a chicken pot pie, red flannel hash or French toast with a vanilla compote.

The newest addition to the restaurant is a wine bar, offering an extensive selection of wines by the glass, and a menu of salads, appetizers and other light fare. Every month, wines of a different style, region or winemaker are featured.

# Mama D's

The real attraction at Mama D's has always been Mama D: Giovanna D'Agostino, a robust Italian woman who started the restaurant in 1965 after her husband died. A large portrait of her hangs in the main dining room and her cookbooks are for sale at the cash register.

Mama D's is and always has been an Italian-American restaurant. That's the nice way of saying that the food comes in two basic colors, red and white, and that vegetables, except for the obligatory iceberg lettuce salad with tomato wedge, are virtually unknown.

This kind of Italian cooking can be done well or badly and on my visits I have found a little bit of each. The highlights include the gnocchi Alfredo, small and dense but tender dumplings made of ricotta, flour and eggs, topped with a light and delicate cheese-flavored cream sauce. The spadini are also excellent — breaded rolls of thinly sliced beef stuffed with mozzarella and ham and topped with a red sauce.

The lasagna is a short-cut version and tasted like it. Instead of the usual multiple layers of meat, noodles and sauce, Mama D's version is more like meatloaf. The flavors all run together and the varied texture of proper lasagna is missing.

The spaghetti and sausage is also a loser. The sauce is about on a par with the standard supermarket brands. The noodles aren't quite al dente and the sausage is also of supermarket grade, mildly seasoned and finely ground.

---

Mama D's
821 Raymond Av.
St Paul
646-7774

4080 W. Broadway
Robbinsdale
537-5147

**HOURS**
St. Paul
M-Th 10:30-8:45
F 10:30-9:45
Sa 4-9:45

Robbinsdale
M-Th 10:30-9
F,Sa 10:30-10
Su 8-10

**PRICES**
$

**CREDIT CARDS**
AE/MC/V/D

**RESERVATIONS**
Recommended

**ATMOSPHERE**
Very casual

**ALCOHOL**
St. Paul: Wine & beer

Robbinsdale: Full bar

# Mama Mia's

**Mama Mia's**
1420 Nicollet Av.
Minneapolis
872-2200

**HOURS**
M-F 11-midnight
Sa 11-1:30 a.m.
Su 12-11:30

**PRICES**
$

**CREDIT CARDS**
AE/MC/V/
CB/DC/D

**RESERVATIONS**
Recommended

**ATMOSPHERE**
Informal

**ALCOHOL**
Wine & beer

I don't want to oversell the place; this is a good restaurant, not a great one, and it does have occasional lapses. But when you're looking for an affordable place to enjoy a glass of wine, a plate of noodles and each other's company, Mama Mia's is worth a try.

Simplicity seems to be the key to Mama Mia's success. There are a half-dozen pasta entrees on the menu, plus occasional specials and a nice selection of appetizers, pizzas and calzone. By sticking to pasta and pizza, Mama Mia's is able to keep prices very reasonable.

All of the appetizers we tried were well-received, but the favorite may have been the fette di melanzane: slices of Italian salami and provolone cheese sandwiched between slices of breaded eggplant, and baked. The Caesar salad, though not classically prepared, is also quite good, but heavy on the anchovies.

Five kinds of pizza are available: traditional thin crust, Chicago-style deep dish, pizza Italiano, calzone (a turnover, with the ingredients on the inside) and a pizza pot pie. The thin-crust pizzas are offered with all the basic pizza toppings such as olives, green peppers and mushrooms, and less traditional choices such as smoked chicken, pineapple, spinach and garlic.

The rotolo verde is a perfect example of how simple ingredients and a little imagination can take the place of expensive ingredients. It's just a homemade noodle dough topped with a thin layer of spinach, pesto and ricotta cheese, sliced into rounds and baked in a tomato basil sauce that has real chunks of tomato and identifiable flecks of basil. Delicious.

The desserts we sampled came from Chez Paul, the French restaurant two doors away. The Italian silk pie, a tall stack of stiff Amaretto chocolate mousse in a pastry crust, is a little rich for my taste but got raves from my companions. The tiramisu, rum-soaked sponge cake with layers of fresh cheese and a dusting of cocoa, got a more mixed review.

# Mancini's

Nick Mancini has built a tremendously successful business on a very simple idea: offering steaks of very good quality in generous portions at a very reasonable price.

Mancini's keeps things simple. You get your choice of sirloin steak, New York steak, beef kebabs, lobster or a steak and lobster combination. And you get a choice of dressing on your iceberg lettuce salad. If you want other choices, you can eat someplace else.

Aside from the fake-log fireplace, Mancini's doesn't have a big investment in decor. Unused chairs are stacked in a corner. Service is on paper placemat maps of Italy atop fake-marble Formica. The sour cream for the baked potato arrives in an airline-style disposable paper carton. But what the customers come for is steak — and value.

On those counts, they're not likely to be disappointed. The steaks I've tried at Mancini's, including a filet and a New York steak, weren't quite as tender as those at fancier steak houses, but they seemed every bit as flavorful — and for half the price.

Dinners are accompanied by a relish tray with pickled cherry peppers, sliced tomatoes and olives.

Mancini's
531 W. 7th St.
St Paul
224-7345

**HOURS**
Su-Sa 5-11

**PRICES**
$

**CREDIT CARDS**
AE/MC/V

**RESERVATIONS**
Recommended

**ATMOSPHERE**
Informal

**ALCOHOL**
Full bar

**ENTERTAINMENT**
Karoake T
Live music W-Sa

## Manny's Steakhouse

**Manny's Steakhouse**
**Hyatt Regency**
**1300 Nicollet Mall,**
**Minneapolis**
**339-9900**

**HOURS**
M-Th 5:30-10
F,Sa 5:30-11
Su 5:30-9

**PRICES**
$$$

**CREDIT CARDS**
AE/MC/V/DC

**RESERVATIONS**
Recommended

**ATMOSPHERE**
Formal/informal

**ALCOHOL**
Full bar

**OTHER**
Small children not encouraged

Manny's steaks are locker-aged for two to four weeks, which makes the meat more tender and flavorful but causes substantial shrinkage, increasing the cost per pound. The sheer size of the portions is staggering. Porterhouse steaks come in 24 or 48 ounces. Pork chops and lamb chops are served 18 ounces to an order. (Splitting orders is permitted.) The smallest cut on the regular menu is a 10-ounce filet mignon.

This kind of eating is more a ritual of conquest than a gastronomic experience. But if your idea of a great evening out is a big juicy steak and a baked potato, served in comfortable surroundings by an extremely professional staff, then you're likely to be thrilled by Manny's.

The starters are traditional, and well-made: sliced smoked salmon, a shrimp cocktail, oysters Rockefeller. My porterhouse was tender and tasty, noticeably more flavorful than the average restaurant steak. A filet mignon was similarly tender and satisfying. A double breast of lemon chicken was nicely seasoned, but rather dry. On a second visit, the grilled veal chop was the best dish we ordered, tender and flavorful. The 2-pound prime rib looks amazing on the plate, but it tasted much like other prime ribs, juicy and reasonably tender.

Salads, potatoes and vegetables must be ordered separately; all are served in portions large enough for two, and are generally very simple dishes, well prepared.

Machismo permeates the place. The walls are hung with photos of bomber squadrons and prints of cowboys. The bathrooms have the marble and brass appointments of a men's club.

**Money-saving tip:** Manny's can be one of the most expensive restaurants in town, especially if your tastes run to lobster or fine French vintages. But you can keep costs down by splitting orders and side dishes or ordering a more affordable steak sandwich or chicken entree.

# Minnesota Zephyr

Minnesota's first dining car train makes a 9-mile run, Thursday through Saturday evenings and Saturday and Sunday afternoons, from Stillwater to Dellwood. The ride offers glimpses of the St. Croix River, a meandering creek, a golf course and some farm fields before delivering you back to Stillwater.

Meal service starts as soon as the train gets rolling. There is no kitchen on board. You select your dinner when you make reservations and the food is prepared and loaded on board. The menu starts with a shrimp cocktail, followed by a chicken and wild rice soup, green salad and then a choice of prime rib, flounder stuffed with crab and lobster, or orange-glazed game hen.

The prime rib, served with a creamy sharp horseradish sauce and accompanied with boiled potatoes, is a very juicy and flavorful piece of meat of generous size and seems not to suffer at all from the advance preparation. Dessert is a delicious chocolate-coated cheesecake.

The Minnesota Zephyr is not the Orient Express. The visual high points include farmland and a well-tended golf course, not breathtaking views of the Alps or mountain villages. And the cuisine, while adequate, is not memorable. There are club cars with upper decks at each end, but not much else to explore on board. But if you're in a suitably romantic or nostalgic mood, you might find that an evening on board the Minnesota Zephyr is just the ticket.

Minnesota Zephyr Limited
601 N. Main
P.O. Box 573
Stillwater
430-3000

**HOURS**
Th-F 6:30
Sa 11:30, 6:30
Su 11:30
(3 hour ride)
Closed
Jan. 1-Feb. 12

**PRICES**
$$$

**CREDIT CARDS**
MC/V/DC

**RESERVATIONS**
Required

**ATMOSPHERE**
Formal

**ALCOHOL**
Full bar

**OTHER**
Limited wheelchair access
Small children not encouraged

# Mirror of Korea

Mirror of Korea
3117 E. Lake St.
Minneapolis
721-3069

**HOURS**
M-Sa 11-9:30

**PRICES**
$

**CREDIT CARDS**
MC/V

**RESERVATIONS**
Recommended

**ATMOSPHERE**
Very casual

**ALCOHOL**
Wine & beer

For adventuresome diners, the Mirror of Korea offers a chance to taste the exotic, sometimes very exotic, cuisine of the Land of the Morning Calm. It doesn't offer much in the way of decor, but the menu is extensive and the prices are very reasonable.

Korean cooking resembles both Chinese and Japanese cooking but has distinctive flavors of its own. Many dishes are fiery hot, though the kitchen will usually oblige when asked for milder renditions. Staple dishes often combine sweet, salty and hot flavors. Aromatic sesame oil and sesame seeds are used in abundance, along with soybean paste, soy sauce, hot pepper sauce and tofu.

Although there is much that might be considered strange in the Korean diet, the Mirror of Korea also has many dishes that even unadventuresome palates are likely to find instantly appealing, such as the bulgogi (flavorful, thinly sliced, broiled beef) or the galbee (a popular dish of marinated broiled short ribs).

Two of the most popular dishes are the dak bok geum and o jing eo bok geum — chicken and cuttlefish, respectively — stir-fried with vegetables in a lively but not overpowering red sauce. More adventuresome palates may wish to try some of the stews and casserole dishes, served piping hot in clay bowls and metal pots.

One of my favorite dishes is naem myung (a big bowl of buckwheat noodles served in a cold, spicy, sour soup, garnished with meat and vegetables). Another favorite is be bim bop (a meal-sized bowl of rice topped with broiled beef, vegetables and fried egg) and an optional very hot sauce.

Dinner entrees are accompanied by seven or eight savory side dishes ranging from kim chee (fiery hot pickled cabbage) and spicy radishes to pickled shreds of cucumber, marinated zucchini, spinach and seaweed.

# Muffuletta

Muffuletta's strong suit is its versatility: You can dine indoors or outdoors (weather permitting) and choose something as simple as a plate of pasta, a sandwich or a chicken pot pie, or splurge on the works: appetizer, soup, primi portion of pasta, and a range of entrees that runs from trout meuniere to steak au poivre.

Preparations are simple and traditional, the quality good. My plate of fettuccine with shrimp, tossed with tomato, garlic, fresh basil and olive oil was a very satisfying dinner and a reminder that dining well doesn't have to mean dining fancy. Other pasta offerings include fettuccine Alfredo, baked ziti with Italian sausage, fusilli with smoked salmon, and several more.

Appetizer options include onion rings, escargot, mussels, calamari and pizzas. Toppings for thick, crisp puffy pies range from Margherita (with tomatoes, goat cheese and fresh basil) to quattro staggioni (with four quarters, topped respectively with artichoke hearts, fresh mushrooms, red peppers and black olives).

The Muffuletta, the restaurant's namesake sandwich and a New Orleans specialty, is a superb onion roll stuffed with salami, mortadella and cheeses and piled high with olives.

One of the most interesting entrees is a tender, moist stuffed chicken breast filled with a flavorful combination of pistachios, walnuts and raisins. The braised beef tips, invariably overcooked and stringy elsewhere, are a pleasant surprise at Muffuletta: lightly cooked chunks of tender beef in a red wine, mushroom and creme fraiche sauce that tastes much like stroganoff, served over homemade fettuccine.

Muffuletta's outdoor patio is one of the nicest in the area. It is well above street level and provides suitable privacy while preserving the feeling of the great outdoors.

---

**Muffuletta
in the Park
2260 Como Av.
St. Paul
644-9116**

**HOURS**
M-F 11:30-3:30, 5-10
Sa 11:30-4:30, 5-10
Su 10:30-2, 5-9

**PRICES**
$

**CREDIT CARDS**
AE/MC/V

**RESERVATIONS**
Recommended

**ATMOSPHERE**
Informal

**ALCOHOL**
Wine & beer

**OTHER**
Limited parking
Sunday buffet brunch

# Murray's

**Murray's Restaurant and Lounge**
26 S. 6th St.
Minneapolis
339-0909

**HOURS**
M-Sa 11-11
Su 4-10

**PRICES**
$$$

**CREDIT CARDS**
AE/MC/V/
CB/DC/D

**RESERVATIONS**
Recommended

**ATMOSPHERE**
Formal

**ALCOHOL**
Full bar

**ENTERTAINMENT**
Musicians M-Sa

For me, a juicy, tender, flavorful steak is a rare treat in more ways than one: the calories, the fat, the cholesterol and the environmental damage done by large-scale meat production are all hard to swallow. Besides which, most steaks don't seem to taste as good as they used to, thanks to the growing American passion for leaner (and thus less flavorful) meat.

So on the rare occasion when I crave steak, I want it to be a really memorable piece of meat. One place that satisfies that desire is Murray's Restaurant and Lounge, which for decades has been the Twin Cities' premier steak house.

Murray's has changed with the times, but not a whole lot. Remodeling has brought the decor into the 1950s, with billowing pink drapes and mirrored walls. Two violins, plus a cello and piano, provide romantic accompaniment. Customers don't come for French haute cuisine; they come for steak, and on that score, Murray's delivers.

The famous silver butter-knife steak for two is a broiled 2-pound chunk roughly the size and shape of a paving stone. It was carved at tableside, and though it wasn't quite tender enough to cut with a butter knife, it was very tender and flavorful, cooked precisely as ordered. The bacon-wrapped filet mignon proved almost too tender, a little mushy around the edges, but still it was an excellent and flavorful piece of meat. The dinner sirloin, which the menu says "emphasizes flavor over tenderness," did have a little gristle, and it was a little chewier than the butter-knife steak, but it was still one of the tastiest I've had in ages.

If I have any beef with Murray's, it's over details. The garlic toast was too greasy and salty — but I couldn't stop eating it. My steak was oversalted as well, as were the French fries.

**Money-saving tip:** The Downtowner menu (served 4 to 6 p.m.) and light dinner menu offer reduced prices.

# My Le Hoa

If restaurant exploring can be compared to bird-watching, then discovering a Chinese restaurant of the caliber of My Le Hoa in a shopping center in Little Canada is the gastronomic equivalent of spotting a cockatoo in the middle of an Iowa cornfield. The menu is the kind you would expect to find in Hong Kong, Toronto or Vancouver, or maybe with great luck in San Francisco or New York. It features such dishes as minced seafood lettuce wrap, barbecued pigeon, baked quail, bird's nest soup, smoked black cod, deep fried duck with lotus taro and ground prawn and bean curd in hot pot.

The appetizer plate of jellyfish, cut into thin, chewy ribbons, and thin slices of skin-on boneless roast pork hock is a delicious combination of textures and flavors, sharply punctuated by a sprinkling of marinated ginger. Also recommended are the roast quail, tiny, coffee-brown birds with a flavor far more intense than chicken or duck.

A nice selection of hot pot dishes is offered, baked in metal pots and brought to the table bubbling hot. The pork with eggplant is prepared with the very tender (and very expensive) pale purple Oriental eggplant. It was a tasty dish, though perhaps a little bland, as was the hot pot of squid and coarsely ground shrimp balls. But I do recommend the house special chow fun, made with soft, fat white rice noodles, tossed with generous quantities of shrimp, scallops, chicken, roast pork and fresh baby bok choy.

The steamed chicken with ginger sauce is served in its own juices with bone in and skin on, hacked into chopstick-sized morsels and topped with matchstick shreds of ginger and scallion. The meat is moist, the flavor delicate. Lobster is prepared several ways; I loved it stir-fried with black bean sauce.

My Le Hoa
2900 Rice St.
Little Canada
484-5353

HOURS
Daily 11:30-10

PRICES
$

CREDIT CARDS
MC/V

RESERVATIONS
Recommended

ATMOSPHERE
Very casual

OTHER
Limited parking
Sunday buffet brunch

# Nankin

**Nankin**
City Center
2 S. 7th St.
Minneapolis
333-3303

HOURS
M-Th 11-3, 5-9
F,Sa 11:30-11:00
Su 12-8

PRICES
$

CREDIT CARDS
AE/MC/V/D

RESERVATIONS
Recommended

ATMOSPHERE
Formal/informal

ALCOHOL
Full bar

OTHER
Sunday buffet brunch

Generations of Minneapolitans grew up on the Nankin's chop suey, chow mein and egg foo young. Now a new generation of diners wants something a little more authentic, so the Nankin strives to please, but without alienating its traditional clientele. The original favorites have been joined by new specialties including Cantonese barbecued duck, moo shu pork and hot and spicy dishes such as Kung Pao chicken, Hunan beef and pork in garlic sauce. (The menu is the same at lunch and dinner.) Judged on its own terms, the traditional Chinese-American isn't bad — the chicken chow mein is properly bland and mushy and the chop suey chow mein combination, made with sliced pork in a thick, dark gravy, is likely to bring back childhood memories of LaChoy and Chun King in a can.

Other dishes are less satisfactory. The pressed duck is a meager amount of unidentifiable meat stuffed with something that tasted a lot like bread crumbs and covered with a generic brown gravy, served over bean sprouts that tasted canned. The shrimp toast and barbecued ribs are extremely greasy and the chicken wings lack seasoning.

If you liked the old Nankin's mushy, mass-produced Chinese-American chow mein, you probably will like the new Nankin. Its specialties aren't very authentic, but they are cooked to order and usually contain an assortment of fresh vegetables. The appetizers and buffet offerings are pretty mediocre. People who want truly authentic Chinese dishes will be much better off elsewhere.

# New French Cafe

While other restaurants stake out claims to elegance or value or romance, the New French Cafe's territory is the avant-garde. The good news for eaters is that underneath all the style and affectation is a lot of genuine culinary substance. The food is smart, imaginative and consistently well-prepared.

In recent years, the menu has taken a turn towards the rustic, with abundant use of root vegetables, kohlrabi, kale, squash, cauliflower and the like. Hors d'oeuvres range from preserved duck on wilted greens to a paté of fall vegetables topped with puff pastry.

The menu features half a dozen entrees, including a roast rack of lamb with basil chevre demiglace, with saffron noodles on a bed of kale and carrots with garlic butter; poached salmon with sorrel cream sauce accompanied by sauteed cucumbers and a steamed summer squash filled with curried acorn squash, and a sauteed duck breast with demiglace of tomato, tarragon, shallots, mushrooms, glazed beets, carrots, onions and wild rice. Prix-fixe multi-course dinners are also featured nightly. The NFC hosts a big annual Bastille Day street party, the second Sunday in July.

**Money-saving tip:** At dinner, the New French Cafe ranks with the most expensive restaurants in town, but there are several more affordable options, including lunch, Saturday and Sunday brunch, Sunday supper, and a late supper on Friday and Saturday nights (10 p.m. to midnight). Lunch selections range from sandwiches and fruit and cheese plates to entrees such as lamb stew with couscous and a fish stew with mussels, salt cod and monkfish in an intense saffron dill cream sauce. Brunch items include omelets, croissants and such main dishes as creamed salt cod with new potatoes and poached chicken breast with a lemon chive cream sauce.

---

**The New French Cafe**
128 N. 4th St.
Minneapolis
338-3790

**HOURS**
M-Th 7 a.m.-9:30 p.m.
F 7 a.m.-midnight
Sa 8 a.m-midnight
Su 8 a.m.-9 p.m.

**PRICES**
$$$

**CREDIT CARDS**
AE/MC/V/DC

**RESERVATIONS**
Recommended

**ATMOSPHERE**
Informal

**ALCOHOL**
Full bar

**OTHER**
Sunday a la carte brunch

# Newport SeaGrill

**Newport SeaGrill**
Riverplace
1 Main St. SE
Minneapolis
378-1338

**HOURS**
M-Sa 11:30-2:30,
5-11
Su 11:30-2:30, 5-10

**PRICES**
$$

**CREDIT CARDS**
AE/MC/V/
CB/DC/D

**RESERVATIONS**
Recommended

**ATMOSPHERE**
Informal

**ALCOHOL**
Full bar

**OTHER**
Sunday buffet
brunch

At the Newport SeaGrill's early predecessor, the Bristol Bar and Grill, I found the food boring and overpriced, and the decor too ordinary to justify the high prices. The SeaGrill is an improvement on all fronts. The menu is more imaginative, the atmosphere more elegant, and while some prices have risen, some are actually lower than several years ago.

The SeaGrill offers a big selection of fresh fish specials nightly, ranging from swordfish and salmon to yellowfin tuna. It also gives diners some more interesting seafood choices, such as peppered shrimp, rigati with sea scallops, cioppino (a seafood stew) and lump crab cakes.

Best bets from the appetizer list are the very fresh oysters on the half shell or the Newport pan roast, a generous portion of shrimp and scallops in a mild but savory chili cream sauce over toasted sourdough bread. The blackened sea scallops with red pepper coulis are too blackened for my taste.

We fared better with our entree selections. The mesquite-grilled swordfish has a firm meaty texture and a very fresh flavor nicely complemented by the beurre blanc sauce, while the poached salmon, tender and delicate, is perfectly matched by an orange citrus sauce. The shrimp and filet combination is simple but satisfying: four large deep-fried shrimp and a sizable chunk of dry-aged beef, of average tenderness but better-than-average flavor.

The Sunday brunch offers a nice spread, including things such as a very tasty crawfish pasta, deviled crab, chicken jambalaya, shrimp Creole and a nice assortment of cold cuts, cheeses, fresh fruit, desserts and breakfast items, as well as omelets made to order.

**Money-saving tip:** During weekday Happy Hour, the downstairs SeaBar features reduced prices on drink and food, including hearty and tasty New England clam chowder and raw oysters.

# Nicollet Island Inn

The Nicollet Island Inn, a handsomely restored hotel just north of downtown Minneapolis, is under new management. The changes include a new chef, Tim Scott, an alum of Goodfellows and the prestigious Culinary Institute of America; and a new menu, emphasizing Minnesota ingredients and dishes.

I won't say that trying to turn Minnesota cooking into haute cuisine is like trying to make a silk purse from a sow's ear (oops, I guess I *did* just say that), but there is always a little danger in these attempts to get fancy with Midwestern cooking. By the time you're done, you have something very tasty but with little resemblance to anything Minnesotans actually eat.

Luckily, the Inn's chefs don't try to get too fancy. The sauteed walleye and scallop cakes actually bear more than a passing resemblance to salmon patties, but they are much more delicate and tasty. The salt- and pepper-cured pan-fried chicken is moist and juicy on the inside, nicely browned on the outside, and much tastier than the deep-fried chicken most restaurants serve these days. Served with the chicken is Lena's hot dish, a classic comfort food casserole of spinach, noodles and several cheeses.

Other menu offerings with a Midwestern flavor include a sesame walleye fillet and a moist and savory Minnesota meatloaf with homemade catsup and mashed potatoes (both available as sandwiches on the lunch menu).

Desserts, such as a white chocolate brownie with homemade ice cream, or a Key lime pie, aren't particularly Midwestern, but they are excellent.

---

**Nicollet Island Inn**
95 Merriam St.
Minneapolis
331-1800

HOURS
M-Th 7 a.m.-10 p.m.
F 7 a.m.-11 p.m.
Sa 8 a.m.-11 p.m.
Su 7 a.m.-9 p.m.

PRICES
$$

CREDIT CARDS
AE/MC/V/CB/DC/D

RESERVATIONS
Recommended

ATMOSPHERE
Formal/informal

ALCOHOL
Full bar

OTHER
Valet parking
Sunday buffet brunch

# Nikki's

**Nikki's Cafe**
107 3rd Av. N.
Minneapolis
340-9098

**HOURS**
Daily 11-11

**PRICES**
$

**CREDIT CARDS**
AE/MC/V/
CB/DC/D

**RESERVATIONS**
Recommended

**ATMOSPHERE**
Informal

**ALCOHOL**
Full bar

**ENTERTAINMENT**
Music nightly

**OTHER**
Limited
wheelchair access
Sunday a la carte
brunch

Nikki's original comfort-food menu of meatloaf, macaroni and cheese and chicken pot pie has shrunk to one small section of the menu, which now also features pizzas, pastas, a wide assortment of appetizers and entrees.

Nikki's cooks roam far afield for their inspiration and come back with dishes that range from a delicious Thai pizza with shrimp, peanut sauce, cilantro and lime to a highly imaginative but virtually inedible combination of fettuccine tossed with beer, sauteed garlic, olive oil, black beans and green onions. More mainline offerings include shrimp scampi or pork medallions with tomato-onion relish and grilled apples.

The quality ranges from wonderful to awful — a superb caponata of eggplant, onions, celery, capers, tomatoes and olives in olive oil, and a miserable Caesar salad drenched in a lemony dressing. The spicy Buffalo chicken wings are absolutely authentic, but the hummus is bland and lifeless. The deep-fried calamari with lemon mayonnaise were snarfed up in milliseconds, while the deep-fried artichoke hearts were deemed adequate, but uninteresting.

The macaroni and cheese, a generous portion of bow-tie pasta with provolone, Swiss and cheddar in a garlic cream sauce, is a very satisfying update on the classic.

Save room for dessert: The apple pie with cinnamon ice cream, crusty bread pudding with bourbon caramel cream sauce and the dessert pizza topped with ice cream, chocolate and caramel sauce and whipped cream are excellent.

Another attraction is the live music performed nightly. Combine that with the relaxed, inviting atmosphere, the reasonable prices and very good food (if you choose carefully) and Nikki's comes out a winner.

# Nye's Polonaise Room

There's nothing the least bit slick or trendy about Nye's Polonaise Room, a Northeast Minneapolis institution. The cuisine and the atmosphere are pretty ordinary. What's special is the character. You're either going to be charmed or you aren't.

Nye's menu combines a handful of Polish specialities with a list of all-American favorites. The restaurant, which has a piano bar, is done up in a sort of imitation-elegance that brings the '50s to mind: lamps of colored glass, red print wallpaper, red patterned carpet and red candle lanterns on the tables.

The gigantic Polonaise plate lets you sample most of the ethnic offerings; it includes Polish sausage, spareribs and sauerkraut, a stuffed cabbage roll, several pierogis and an enormous potato dumpling. The sauerkraut is poetry — cooked for hours with the spareribs so that it loses the sharpness of its raw state and absorbs the flavors of the meat. The accompanying spareribs are meaty and flavorful, the meat so tender it falls off the bone. The pierogi (pockets of dough stuffed with mashed potatoes, cheese or prune jam) are satisfactory renditions, but the potato dumpling is as heavy as a cannonball.

Other dishes are less satisfactory. The roast duck is quite overcooked, its skin limp and greasy, its orange sauce dull. The prime rib is a generous cut that seemed to have been sliced well in advance of my order; not bad, but not as tender as the best. The chicken Kiev is so perfectly shaped and evenly breaded that it aroused suspicions, which our waitress quickly confirmed: It was store-bought.

On a lunchtime visit, I sampled the barbecued spareribs, which had been baked for a very long time; what flavor remained had been drowned out by a sharp barbecue sauce.

Nye's Bar
& Polonaise Room
112 E. Hennepin
Minneapolis
379-2021

HOURS
M-Sa 11 a.m.-1 a.m.

PRICES
$

CREDIT CARDS
AE/MC/V/DC

RESERVATIONS
Recommended

ATMOSPHERE
Informal

ALCOHOL
Full bar

OTHER
Limited wheelchair access
Piano bar M-Sa, dancing F,S

## Odaa

**Odaa Ethiopian Restaurant**
408 Cedar Av.
Minneapolis
338-4459

HOURS
M-Th 11-10
F,Sa 11-11
Su 3-9

PRICES
$

CREDIT CARDS
AE/MC/V

RESERVATIONS
Recommended

ATMOSPHERE
Informal

ALCOHOL
Beer

Eating Ethiopian-style is one of the most unusual and enjoyable dining experiences you can have locally. Cutlery is optional.

Everyone eats with their hands from the same tray covered with a layer of soft pancake-like bread and then topped with a choice from a wide variety of mild or spicy beef, lamb, chicken or vegetarian dishes. You tear off chunks of the bread and use it to scoop up morsels of the meat and vegetables.

If you really want to follow tradition, you place the food in your companion's mouth, rather than your own, and they in turn feed you. (Hand-washing before meals is also an important Ethiopian custom.)

The Odaa sampler lets you try three different meats, as well as all of the meatless dishes featured in the vegetarian sampler, including flavorful stews of yellow split peas; green lentils; cabbage, carrots and potatoes, and green beans and carrots; red lentils; fava beans; collard greens, and two yogurt sauces. Initial portions are generous and unlimited seconds are available on most of the dishes.

Try a mango sundae for dessert and steamed Ethiopian coffee or tea or a mango shake.

The modest but attractive decor includes recreations of a round house and shelter buildings commonly used by the Oromo people of Ethiopia.

# Origami

You're more likely to enjoy a visit to Origami if you know what to expect. This is a problem only because Origami bills itself as Japanese-French, which it is not. The menu has a couple of appetizers with pseudo-French names, such as croquette de crab and coquille de scallop, but neither of these is remotely French.

Most of what the menu offers is typical Japanese restaurant fare: sushi, sashimi, tempura and grilled fish, plus lots of versions of beef and chicken with teriyaki sauce, chicken kebabs, beef kebabs, teriyaki chicken and Kobe-style steak. But much of the traditional Japanese restaurant repertoire is missing. There is no sukiyaki, no shabu-shabu, no tonkatsu (breaded pork cutlet) or chawan-mushi (seafood and egg custard).

Instead, the menu reaches beyond the usual repertoire by offering such entrees as grilled Alaskan halibut with mushroom sauce, chilled steamed chicken with a spicy sesame seed sauce and an unusual seafood casserole.

The other striking differences from the usual Japanese restaurant are the service and ambience. Origami has a bistro feel, with a color scheme of pale blue, purple and lavender and original Haitian art on the walls.

What Origami does with food, it does pretty well, though quality is occasionally uneven. The raw fish, served in the various sashimi and sushi dishes, is consistently very fresh. The tempura is excellent: a generous serving of crisp batter-fried shrimp and assorted veggies.

The Encounter appears to be an Origami original. At least, I have never seen anyone else attempt to dip a sushi roll in tempura batter and deep fry it. The result is very satisfying. The filling of salmon, scallops, avocado, pickled ginger and pickled burdock is a tasty combination of flavors and textures.

Dessert offerings include vanilla ice cream topped with sweet adzuki beans and green tea ice cream.

---

**Origami**
30 N 1st St.
Minneapolis
333-8430

**HOURS**
M-Th 11:30-2:30, 5-10
F 11:30-2:30, 5-12
Sa 5-12

**PRICES**
$$

**CREDIT CARDS**
AE/MC/V/DC

**RESERVATIONS**
Required

**ATMOSPHERE**
Informal

**ALCOHOL**
Full bar

**OTHER**
Limited parking
Small children not encouraged

# Pickled Parrot

**Pickled Parrot**
26 N. 5th St.
Minneapolis
332-0673

**HOURS**
Daily 11-1 a.m.

**PRICES**
$

**CREDIT CARDS**
AE/MC/V

**RESERVATIONS**
Recommended

**ATMOSPHERE**
Formal/informal

**ALCOHOL**
Full bar

**ENTERTAINMENT**
Live music and dance

**OTHER**
Limited wheelchair access
Limited parking

The Pickled Parrot is a flashy bar and restaurant with Southern, Tex-Mex and Caribbean accents. In culinary terms this translates into chili peppers, barbecue and tropical fruit. For decor there's a giant papier-mache swordfish placed high overhead, but not in the usual taxidermist's mount. The tail sticks out of the wall, the midsection disappears into it and the head sticks out a few feet away.

The menu-planners also obviously had a good time: Combinations include a nopal cactus salad topped with pumpkin seeds and chili-pepper vinaigrette, a soup of the day that combines shrimp and bananas and entrees such as chicken with papaya mint salsa and a warm lobster taco. The ideas are fine; the execution is sometimes uneven.

A couple of the highly recommended entrees also show up as appetizers: the baby back ribs and the red chile pasta with crab. I can also recommend both the chile verde and the chicken chili. The first is a rich, spicy soup of beef, lamb, chicken and bacon (with no trace of green chiles), while the latter is more of a grilled chicken dish with black beans in it than a bean dish with chicken.

The Pickled Parrot's version of fajitas are attractively presented but short on flavor. For big meat eaters, there's a cowboy plate: A sizable chunk of sirloin topped with sauteed mushrooms and onions and two good-sized pork chops.

Your best bet might be to skip the entrees and opt instead for one of the sandwiches. The combination of grilled tuna steak and cilantro-pumpkin-seed pesto works very well. Also recommended is the Santa Fe Club sandwich, a grilled chicken breast topped with black bean sauce, chipotle pepper sauce and bacon.

Desserts include a very solid caramel nut pie full of macadamias and cashews and a moist, nutty carrot cake. Service is friendly and laid-back, but reasonably prompt. A nice selection of micro-brewery and imported beers is offered.

# Polo Italia

Polo Italia has lived up to its potential by paying attention to the little things. While earlier visits found the cuisine and the service were no match for the decor and ambitious menu, the kitchen now is more careful about the details: The pasta is served properly al dente and there is plenty of strong garlic and basil cream sauce to bathe the steamed mussels.

The bruschetta (grilled Italian bread topped with marinated tomatoes) has a good balance of garlic, chopped tomatoes, onions, oil and basil. The calamari fritti (fried squid) are nicely crisp and chewy, served with a lively marinara sauce.

The entrees were also well received. A marinated steak, offered as a nightly special, is generous and flavorful, and a grilled tuna steak with fresh herbs is equally satisfying. The chicken saltimbocca is a hit: a generous double breast, topped with prosciutto ham and romano cheese and sauteed with artichoke hearts. The vegetarian dish of cappelini pasta with artichoke hearts, broccoli and goat cheese in a tomato cream sauce was much too bland.

Vegetarians have a number of other options on the Polo Italia menu, including the spaghettini pomodoro (with roma tomatoes, garlic, basil and red onion); a linguini al pesto, made with basil and pine nuts, and several pizzas.

Portions are generous; among the four of us, we could find room enough to share only one selection from the dessert tray, and opted for the tiramisu (liqueur-soaked ladyfingers topped with mascarpone cheese and cocoa), an excellent rendition of an Italian classic.

The bar at Polo Italia has been renamed "Apple Pie: American Foods, Spirits, etc." and now serves a low-priced menu of burgers, sandwiches, salads and comfort foods such as meat loaf and chicken pot pie.

---

**Polo Italia**
9920 Wayzata Bvd.
St. Louis Park
545-0041

**HOURS**
M-Th 11:30-10
F 11:30-11
S 5-11
Su 3-10

**PRICES**
$

**CREDIT CARDS**
AE/MC/V/CB/DC/D

**RESERVATIONS**
Recommended

**ATMOSPHERE**
Informal

**ALCOHOL**
Full bar

**ENTERTAINMENT**
DJ F,Sa

**OTHER**
Limited parking

# Pronto

☆

**Pronto Ristorante and Caffe Pronto**
Hyatt Regency
1300 Nicollet Mall
Minneapolis
333-4414

**HOURS**
M-Th 11:30-10
F 11:30-11
Sa 5-11 Su 4-9

**PRICES**
Restaurant $$
Cafe $

**CREDIT CARDS**
AE/MC/V

**RESERVATIONS**
Recommended

**ATMOSPHERE**
Formal/informal

**ALCOHOL**
Full bar

**OTHER**
Limited wheelchair access
Small children not encouraged

❧

Pronto, on the concourse level of the Hyatt Regency in downtown Minneapolis, is really two restaurants: the elegant and expensive Pronto Ristorante, with white tablecloths and romantic lighting, and the casual affordable Caffe Pronto. While Pronto Ristorante offers a complete selection of *antipasti, insalate, primi* and *secondi,* Caffe Pronto offers down-to-earth prices for a more basic menu of pizzas, pastas and a few grilled entrees. At the Caffe, you can have a plate of pasta and a glass of house wine for about $10 in very attractive surroundings: a white tile interior, tiered seating and an open kitchen.

Perhaps the best value at Caffe Pronto is the *piccolo* (small) serving of the assorted appetizer plate. The selection varies but can include Italian salami and cheeses, marinated fava beans, prepared salads, sliced tomato with fresh mozzarella, figs, sometimes stuffed mussels, marinated mushrooms and fresh slices of melon wrapped with prosciutto, all accompanied by bread and fruity herbed olive oil.

The Caffe's thin-crust pizzas include a few more traditional renditions, but the rest of the list ranges from the gamberetti di coco (topped with shrimp, toasted coconut and red and green peppers), to the pollo picante (chicken breast and spicy ginger, peanut and sesame sauce).

The selections of pastas, which are somewhat different at Caffe Pronto and Pronto Ristorante, also range from spaghetti Napoletana and fettuccine Alfredo to ravioli filled with acorn squash and tossed with Parmesan, cream, pears and walnuts.

The Caffe Pronto also features half a dozen entrees, ranging from grilled swordfish alla caponata and veal scallopini to broiled salmon, while the Ristorante features a more extensive list of higher-priced *secondi.*

**Money-saving tip:** In the elegant Ristorante, instead of meat or poultry, order an entree-sized portion of pasta ($3 extra.)

# Quail on the Hill

Quail on the Hill has answered complaints that its cuisine and decor didn't justify its prices with a two-pronged response: Chef Christian Caille has improved the ambience and introduced less-expensive entrees and dinner specials. The additions include such rustic French country dishes as boudin blanc (a pork-and-chicken sausage served with sauteed apples and onion), cassoulet (a casserole of beans, sausage and pork) and carbonnade Flamande (beef cooked in beer).

The onion soup has plenty of flavorful broth, while the appetizer combination of snails, garlic and artichoke hearts works well. The cocktail Cote d'Azur mixes shrimp, hearts of palm and grapefruit sections with a pink mayonnaise; the grapefruit provided the perfect balance to the richness of the sauce and shrimp.

The nightly four-course prix fixe special is an excellent value. My sample included cream of lettuce soup that wasn't really a cream soup at all but a flavorful, slightly salty and much less caloric broth of pureed lettuce in chicken stock. The alternative, a Caesar-like salad of crisp romaine lettuce, was excellent. The appetizer was a smaller portion of the nightly special, firm and fresh poached salmon with a delicious tomato-saffron Provencale sauce.

Among the entrees, the confit of duck is remarkably tender and flavorful. The scampi are plump and juicy, but the accompanying sauce is too bland. Seafood on a shell turns out to be not a pastry shell but a medley of shrimp, fish and scallops in Provencale sauce on an inedible scallop shell. The most popular entree with my companions combines a small filet mignon in a cognac sauce with a semi-boneless stuffed quail in a red wine sauce, both savory and tender.

Desserts include crisp homemade profiteroles filled with ice cream and topped with chocolate sauce, ordinary but agreeable creme caramel and a bete noire (a rich and dense flourless chocolate cake).

**Quail on the Hill**
371 Selby Av.
St. Paul
291-1236

HOURS
M-F 11:30-10:30
Sa 5:30-10:30

PRICES
$$

CREDIT CARDS
MC/V

RESERVATIONS
Recommended

ATMOSPHERE
Informal

ALCOHOL
Wine & beer

ENTERTAINMENT
Classical music F, French singer every other Sa

OTHER
Small children not encouraged

# Rainbow Chinese

☆

Rainbow Chinese
Restaurant
2750 S. Nicollet
Minneapolis
870-7084

HOURS
M-Th 11:30-10
F,Sa 11:30-2 a.m.
Su 11:30-9

PRICES
$

CREDIT CARDS
AE/MC/V

RESERVATIONS
Recommended

ATMOSPHERE
Informal

ALCOHOL
Wine & beer

⚜

The Rainbow Chinese Restaurant, tucked away in a strip mall of Oriental businesses, has gradually been transformed from a modest little noodle house into a first-rate Cantonese cafe, with a full menu of Cantonese specialties, and seafood specials on weekends.

The menu isn't as extensive as at My Le Hoa or the Village Wok, but for the gastronomic thrill-seeker there's no shortage of novelties. Alongside the familiar Hunan beef, Kung Pao chicken and shrimp with lobster sauce, you'll find such unusual dishes as squid with salted vegetable and Eight Treasure rice pudding.

One of the most unusual is the sliced duckling with ginger root (tasty, chewy, small slices of tender meat and crisp roasted skin stir-fried with zesty slices of pink pickled ginger). One of the best and most unusual of the spicier dishes is the Szechuan-style shrimp with spiced pepper; it offers a generous quantity of large shrimp tossed with green pepper and onion in a peppery dark sauce faintly reminiscent of Creole gravies.

The simplest dishes are probably the Rainbow's strongest suit: bowls of noodles in soup, simple plates of rice topped with barbecued chicken, duck or pork, and even simpler, a basic plate of pan-fried fresh noodles topped with slivers of ginger and scallion and laced with a little oyster sauce. In this category, I can recommend the Chiu Chow rice sticks and noodles in soup (a meal-sized bowl of broth brimming with noodles and garnished with an assortment of seafoods and barbecued pork).

# Ristorante Luci

Ristorante Luci is the kind of simple, small, friendly restaurant that adds something to the quality of life in the neighborhood. The tiny cafe has only a dozen tables in its crowded dining room, so reservations are a must.

The menu concentrates on doing a few things well. Six antipasti and a soup of the day are listed, plus a choice of ten pastas and seven meat, poultry and fish entrees, including pork scallopini, grilled chicken breast and veal Marsala. Daily pasta and fish specials also are offered. The reasonably priced pastas include such dishes as spaghetti with olive oil, garlic and red pepper, or fresh fettuccine with button, porcini and oyster mushrooms. The penne all'Amatriciana consists of short tubular noodles tossed with chunks of smoked bacon, sauteed onion, Romano cheese and ripe tomato. The smoky flavor of the bacon permeates the dish but doesn't overwhelm it and the chewy texture contrasted nicely with the pasta and tomato.

On my first visit, the daily taster's dinner included an antipasto of roasted marinated red peppers (obviously homemade) with finely diced zucchini, a shocking pink cream of beet soup, the house salad, homemade gnocchi (potato dumplings) in a sage butter and a modest portion of very fresh steamed halibut in a citrus butter sauce. (It's now just four courses; you get a choice of soup or salad.) On a return trip, dinner included a soup of red bell peppers and winter vegetables in chicken stock, thinly sliced calamari tossed with grapefruit and leeks, a mouthwatering combination of hollow penne noodles with pecans, broccoli, mushrooms and a tantalizing hint of Gorgonzola, and a fish course of salmon with a herb butter.

The fare may be simple, but much attention is given to details. The fettuccine and tagliatelle are made from scratch on the premises, and the servers grate fresh Parmesan and Romano over your pasta. The overall experience is very enjoyable.

☆

**Ristorante Luci**
470 S. Cleveland
St. Paul
699-8258

HOURS
M-Th 5-9:30
F,Sa 5-10:30

PRICES
$

CREDIT CARDS
None

RESERVATIONS
Required

ATMOSPHERE
Informal

ALCOHOL
Wine & beer

OTHER
Limited wheelchair access

## Rossini's Trattoria

**HOURS**
M-F 7-4, 5-10
Sa 11-10

**PRICES**
$

**CREDIT CARDS**
MC/V

**RESERVATIONS**
Recommended

**ATMOSPHERE**
Informal

**ALCOHOL**
Wine & beer

Rossini's Trattoria has all of the makings of a good Italian restaurant, except one. It has well-prepared and mostly authentic Italian cuisine, reasonable prices, a nice selection of Italian wines and such charming touches as fresh flowers and real tablecloths (covered by butcher paper). The only catch is the setting, on the ground level of the Centennial Lakes Medical Building, with a size and layout that make the place look more like a mall deli than a serious restaurant.

Which makes the quality of the food a pleasant surprise — somebody in the kitchen certainly knows how to cook.

The spaghetti carbonara tastes like the genuine article — beaten eggs, pancetta and Parmesan, cooked in the heat of the freshly boiled pasta. The chicken cacciatore, made with whole black olives and carrots, is a robust dish, more flavorful than the usual restaurant renditions. The porchetta, tender boneless pork sauteed with mushrooms, green peppers and black olives, is flavorful without being at all spicy.

There were a few disappointments: the insalata caprese, which in its best and most authentic renditions combines fresh basil, fresh goat cheese, and ripe summer tomatoes in a cold salad, was served hot, with melted cheese over quartered hard tomatoes. The pizza Margherita was not a whole pie, but three wedges, topped with tomato, basil and sliced hard-boiled egg.

There's more on the menu that I would like to try, including the spaghetti alla Napoletana (with fresh tomato sauce), the polenta with sausage and peppers and the pepper steak.

# Royal Orchid

The Royal Orchid is one of the best Thai restaurants in the Twin Cities, but because of its location, it doesn't attract the crowds that it deserves. Start your meal with the mieng kham (a do-it-yourself appetizer of small lettuce leaves that serve as wrappers for an assortment of fillers including roasted peanuts, dried shrimp, diced ginger, diced limes, toasted coconut and tiny but potent shreds of fresh Thai hot pepper). Other appetizers are equally satisfying: tohd mon (four flavorful patties of chopped fish and thinly sliced green beans deep fried and served with a spicy sauce); angel wing (a large chicken wing stuffed with a savory blend of cellophane noodles and finely chopped water chestnuts).

The yum rah yong salad has squid rings deep-fried to a crunchy golden brown and tossed with peanuts, onion, coriander and deep-fried bits of fish maw, which have the same light texture as deep-fried pork rinds. Another salad, of shrimp with lemon grass, hot pepper, lime juice and mint leaves, arrives very lightly cooked, the small pieces of shrimp moist and permeated with the flavors of the lemon grass and spices.

Among my favorite entrees are the red curry roast duck (very tender pieces of long-cooked duck with slices of bamboo shoot in a savory coconut milk sauce flavored with slices of jalapeno pepper) and the yellow chicken gaeng krah rhie (a spicy brown sauce, also made with a coconut milk base, and a blend of spices I can only guess at: red pepper, galangal, lemon grass, turmeric and perhaps ginger). In most cases sauces aren't bland, but they're kept within reach of nearly every palate.

Desserts offer some options rarely seen in these parts. Taro root ice cream from Thailand has a flavor a little like coconut, the Thai custard is soggy and over-sweet, but a plate of mango with sticky rice is a real treat.

A good and reasonably priced buffet is featured at lunch.

☆

Royal Orchid
1835 S. Nicollet
Minneapolis
872-1938

**HOURS**
T-Th 11-10
F 11-11
Sa 12-11
Su 12-10

**PRICES**

**CREDIT CARDS**
MC/V/D

**RESERVATIONS**
Recommended

**ATMOSPHERE**
Informal

**ALCOHOL**
Wine & beer

# Ruam Mit Thai

Ruam Mit Thai
Cafe
544 St. Peter St.
St. Paul
290-0067

HOURS
M-Th 11-10
F,Sa 11-11
Su 3-9

PRICES
$

CREDIT CARDS
None

RESERVATIONS
Recommended

ATMOSPHERE
Very casual

ALCOHOL
None

OTHER
Limited parking

The Ruam Mit Thai Cafe offers excellent value in an out-of-the-way St. Paul location. The prices are a bargain and although the quality of the food arguably should keep the place packed, it's small enough so that the owner will never become rich and distant.

Best bets include the miang kham appetizer, an attractively presented plate of diced lime, onion and ginger, roasted peanuts, chopped jalapenos, toasted coconut and dried shrimp. You take a pinch of each, stuff it into a lettuce leaf and dip it into a sweet and spicy sauce. The young bamboo shoots stuffed with pork and black mushrooms are a little woody, but tasty and quite unusual, as is the banh xeo, a golden rice flour pancake stuffed with your choice of pork, chicken or shrimp.

Of the entrees, my favorites include the roast duck curry, prepared with peas and basil in a rich red coconut milk sauce, the matsman curry, a savory brown stew of beef, potatoes and peanuts, and the papaya salad, a medley of grated unripe papaya, chopped tomatoes, dried shrimp, red pepper, garlic and fish sauce, served with a crisp dry beef jerky, lettuce and a basket of steamed sticky rice.

# St. Paul Grill

I've been to the St. Paul Grill in the St. Paul Hotel on several occasions, and I'm still not persuaded that anybody in the kitchen has any great talent for cooking. The funny thing is, I like the place all the same. In fact, I like it a lot.

Of course, you don't really have to be a superb cook to turn out a juicy, well-grilled piece of fish or steak, or a first-rate roast beef hash. And you certainly don't have to know how to cook to create an atmosphere that's friendly and inviting. Those are the St. Paul Grill's strong suits: simple dishes well-prepared and served in an attractive and comfortable setting. Mahogany paneling, art-deco light fixtures and potted palms give the restaurant a classic but not stuffy ambience.

The St. Paul Grill tries to offer something for nearly everyone. For meat-and-potato types, there's a nice selection of steaks and chops. For diners who want something a little more sophisticated, offerings include wild-mushroom strudel, tequila shrimp with citrus butter sauce and chicken fettuccine with garlic cream sauce. (These more ambitious dishes aren't always successful, but at least they have been tried.)

An appetizer order of cold-smoked salmon (smoked on the premises) is also a pleasant surprise — a more intensely smoky flavor than most of the imported varieties, but still with enough of the buttery texture of uncooked salmon.

Desserts are simple but satisfying. My favorites include a deep-dish apple pie served with Sebastian Joe's cinnamon ice cream and a chocolate mousse liberally laced with Bailey's Irish Cream.

The Sunday brunch is also recommended. Selections include both breakfast items such as tenderloin eggs Benedict and a seafood omelet and lunch items such as a steak scampi and crab cakes. Prices include a glass of champagne or orange juice and a plate of fresh fruit with Devonshire cream.

---

St. Paul Grill
St. Paul Hotel
350 Market St.
St. Paul
224-7455

**HOURS**
M 11:30-10
T-Sa 11:30-11
Su 10-10
Bar menu daily 2-12

**PRICES**
$$

**CREDIT CARDS**
AE/MC/V/CB/DC/D

**ATMOSPHERE**
Informal

**ALCOHOL**
Wine & beer

# Sakura

Sakura Restaurant
& Fish Market
Galtier Plaza
175 E. 5th St.
St. Paul
224-0185

HOURS
M-Th 11-2:30,
4:30-9
F,Sa 11-2:30,
4:30-10
Su 2-9

PRICES
$

CREDIT CARDS
AE/MC/V
CB/DC/D

RESERVATIONS
Recommended

ATMOSPHERE
Informal

ALCOHOL
Wine & beer

The first time I visited Sakura, my companion and I arrived nearly at closing time. We were soon the only customers, but service is friendly and unhurried. The owner (Miyoko Omori, I later learned) stopped by several times, first to make sure everything was all right, then to offer a sample of stew and finally just to talk.

Winners among the warm appetizers include broiled marinated beef ribs and the gyoza (pan fried dumplings filled with pork). The cold appetizer selection includes sashimi: a few slices each of raw tuna, yellowtail, mackerel and boiled octopus, handsomely presented on a wooden tray with wasabe (green horseradish paste) and pickled ginger. The raw fish is fresh enough to be enjoyable, but not at its peak. (Sashimi in Minnesota seldom is). Better bets include the gama-ae (quickly boiled spinach with a savory sesame sauce) and the oshinko (a portion of salty pickled cucumber and radish), which seems intended to go with beer.

Most of the entrees are familiar Japanese fare: a couple of sushi platters, a choice of shrimp, seafood, chicken or vegetable tempura; chicken, salmon, swordfish or beef teriyaki; plus sukiyaki and yosenabe (a seafood soup).

The shogun bento combination offers a few pieces of crisp, lightly breaded shrimp and vegetable tempura, tasty morsels of marinated beef teriyaki, pieces of tuna, yellowtail and mackerel sashimi and some lightly sauteed vegetables. The delightful salmon teriyaki is a generous portion of fresh broiled fish basted with the traditional sweet and salty sauce. The yosenabe is a pleasant medley of scallops, crab legs, green-lipped mussels and a shrimp with spinach, onions, carrots, bean thread noodles and bamboo shoots in a seafood broth.

Devotees of Japanese cuisine probably won't be impressed by the range or standards of Sakura's cuisine, but prices are very reasonable, portions generous and service friendly and attentive.

# Samurai Steak House

The Samurai is a teppanyaki place, an American creation where the chef does chop-chop at your table. Parties of eight are seated around a table-size grill, and the chef cooks the meal as you watch.

As teppanyaki creator Rocky Aoki once explained, "Americans enjoy eating in exotic surroundings but are deeply distrustful of exotic foods." So what he came up with is good old Middle American steak, chicken and shrimp, plus lobster and scallops, very blandly seasoned, cooked with a lot of showmanship on a hot grill. The Samurai is a lower-budget version of this format, minus some of the charm.

The dinner starts with a bowl of thin onion broth with a slice or two of scallion and raw mushroom in it, followed by an iceberg lettuce salad topped with a ginger dressing. The chef arrives, bows and proceeds to the appetizer — a choice of chicken livers or shrimp. Nearly everybody seems to pick the shrimp, which the chef quickly cooks on the hot grill and then deftly cuts into small pieces.

The main courses include a choice of sesame chicken, shrimp, strip steak, sirloin or filet mignon, plus a couple of combinations including scallops and lobster. Except for the scallops, these are also chopped into bite-sized pieces and seasoned with a soy-based sauce. Fried rice and veggies are cooked on the grill, seasoned the same way, more or less, and then portioned out.

What happens when you prepare and season everything the same way? It all comes out tasting pretty much the same. My warrior steak — a New York strip — was quite tender and tasty, but other steaks we tried were less satisfying. And the technique doesn't work well at all on scallops or lobster, both of which turned out rather dry, as did the sesame chicken.

The Samurai is selling an experience, rather than a meal. But even at that, it lacked much of the banter and showmanship I've seen at other teppanyaki restaurants.

---

**Samurai Steak House**
850 S. Louisiana
Golden Valley
542-9922

**HOURS**
M-Th 5-10
F,Sa 5-11
Su 4:30-9

**PRICES**

**CREDIT CARDS**
AE/MC/V/
CB/DC/D

**RESERVATIONS**
Recommended

**ATMOSPHERE**
Informal

**ALCOHOL**
Full bar

# Sawatdee

**Sawatdee**
607 Washington
Av. S.
Minneapolis
338-6451

289 E. 5th St.
St. Paul
222-5859

8501 Lyndale Av.
Bloomington
888-7177

**HOURS**
Su-Th 11-10
F,Sa 11-11

**PRICES**
$

**CREDIT CARDS**
AE/MC/V/
CB/DC/D

**RESERVATIONS**
Recommended

**ATMOSPHERE**
Informal

**ALCOHOL**
Full bar

**OTHER**
Limited parking
Small children
not encouraged
Sunday a la carte
brunch

Sawatdee offers a wide selection of Thai dishes to explore, and the best way to enjoy it is with a crowd: Order lots of everything and pass it around.

The best appetizers include the fresh spring rolls wrapped in rice paper and filled with pork, shrimp, rice noodles, coriander and mint and served with a sweet sauce flecked with chopped peanuts. The paradise chicken wings, stuffed with a well-seasoned mixture of pork, water chestnuts, cellophane noodles and mushrooms, also got an enthusiastic reception. We were less fond of the Thai crispy noodles, a pile of deep-fried noodles tossed with shrimp, fried egg and tofu in a cloyingly sweet sauce.

Most of the spicier dishes can be ordered mild, medium or hot, but they don't always arrive that way. On one visit, I ordered a red chicken curry (simmered in coconut milk with bamboo shoots and green peppers) medium hot, and it arrived rather mild; on another try, a dish of silver thread noodle salad with pork, shrimp and mint leaves, ordered medium, was almost unbearably hot. The vegetarian hot and sour soup is available only hot; it is not for the faint of heart. The only other dish I ordered hot, chicken holy basil supreme (sauteed with onions, mushrooms, hot pepper and basil), was simply too spicy for me, and my tolerance is relatively high. If you overdo it, you can put out the fire with a fresh mango shake or a bottle of Thai Singha beer.

Thai curries are very different from Indian curries. In Sawatdee's curries, the sauces are rich and complex, but the meat is sometimes overcooked. An excellent alternative is the Rama Thai delight, large sauteed shrimp sliced in half and served in a rich peanut curry and coconut-milk sauce over a bed of steamed spinach. I was rather less excited about the Thai roast duck, which had firm but rather dry meat and a skin permeated with the flavor of black bean sauce.

# Scully's

While it isn't as good as it could be, Scully's is a welcome addition to the local restaurant scene, especially the scene around I-494.

In a landscape cluttered with chain restaurants and over-priced hotel eateries, Scully's offers imaginative, reasonably priced, mostly well-prepared cooking.

A wide assortment of pasta dishes is offered, and the thick, crusty, dinner-sized pizzas range from the traditional to a more unusual topping of smoked chicken, sage and fontina.

You can order your choice of broiled trout with tarragon butter, trout stuffed with bay shrimp and fontina, or half a rotisserie chicken.

The chef has an eclectic palate. He's equally at home with Italian pastas and pizzas, Korean grilled ribs and chicken wings, Thai skewers of satay chicken, Japanese yaki soba noodles in a spicy peanut sauce or good old American cheeseburgers.

Be sure to save room for dessert — a banana split if you can manage it. The ice cream is supplied by Sebastian Joe's, an excellent local ice cream company, and the banana split comes topped with chocolate sauce, raspberry Chambord liqueur sauce and toasted pecans. A strawberry rhubarb pie, served as a nightly special, is also highly recommended; the apple pecan cake is not.

Scully's has a casual, attractive decor with lots of natural woodwork and a nautical motif. A couple of large-screen TVs in the bar are visible throughout the main dining room. Smokers and nonsmokers are well separated.

**Scully's Broiler & Bar**
1321 E. 78th St.
Bloomington
854-0107

**HOURS**
M-Th 6 a.m.-11 p.m.
F 6 a.m.-midnight
Sa 7 a.m.-midnight
Su 7 a.m.-10 p.m.

**PRICES**
$

**CREDIT CARDS**
AE/MC/V/DC

**ATMOSPHERE**
Informal

**ALCOHOL**
Full bar

**OTHER**
Sunday a la carte brunch

# Sherlock's Home

**Sherlock's Home**
11000 Red Circle Dr.
Minnetonka
931-0203

**HOURS**
M-Th 11-10
F,Sa 11-11
Su 4-10

**PRICES**
$$

**CREDIT CARDS**
AE/MC/V/DC

**RESERVATIONS**
Recommended

**ATMOSPHERE**
Informal

**ALCOHOL**
Full bar

Sherlock's Home Brewery has the look and feel of a real English pub along with pub grub such as Scotch eggs, toad in the hole or fish 'n' chips.

But the real draws here are the authentic British ales brewed on the premises. The Bishop's Bitter is an excellent rendition of an English bitter, while the Piper's Pride is made in the darker, sweeter style of Scottish ale. The Palace Porter is a darker, heavier brew, but not as heavy as the Stag's Head stout, an Irish-style that tastes like a fresher, livelier version of Guinness Stout.

Typical fare includes a good ploughman's lunch, Welsh rarebit and cock-a-leekie (a Scottish chicken and leek soup). There also are salads, a pasta entree and a few more elegant entrees such as sea scallops Bretonne, chicken breast diablo, salmon fillet Victoria and pork medallions in lemon caper sauce. The cook apparently has a taste for curry; the menu includes generous appetizers of coronation chicken and seafood kedgeree and a dinner entree of savory curried lamb with pappadums. And of course, there is that epitome of English food, roast beef and Yorkshire pudding.

Although British cooking has a terrible reputation, the quality at Sherlock's is quite good. The battered fish was firm, tasty and not greasy. The delicate sea scallops were very fresh and large, cooked not a minute too long and complemented by a light sauce. This food is solidly, stolidly British: thick lamb chops, juicy roast beef, a delightfully moist and tender semiboneless pheasant. True to the British reputation, the asparagus was just a little overcooked. The desserts, served from a trolley, are superb.

# Shilla

The Shilla restaurant doubles as a Korean cocktail lounge with a large-screen TV for playing karaoke (sing-along instrumental music videos, recorded minus vocals). It's good enough to be worth a visit.

A stir-fry of octopus with onions, carrots, scallions, green pepper is delicious, but extremely hot and spicy. The kimchee chigay casserole, a big earthenware soup of spiced cabbage, pork, tofu, carrots and onions, is less fiery, but still quite hot, as is the corvina casserole, which includes a modest quantity of fish in a spicy broth with clams, tofu, scallions and other vegetables.

The Shilla Jongshik, billed as a home-style Korean dinner, is a good place for those new to Korean food. It includes galbee (very tasty grilled marinated beef ribs), as well as a soup of tofu, cabbage and clams, rice and the assorted namul plates of seasoned vegetables. Appetizer orders of mandoo dumplings and bin dae kuk (mung bean pancakes) are excellent, but really unnecessary given the size of the other portions.

Shilla Stone BBQ
694 N. Snelling
St. Paul
645-0006

**HOURS**
T-Sa 11-10
Su 12-9

**PRICES**
$

**CREDIT CARDS**
None

**ATMOSPHERE**
Very casual

**ALCOHOL**
Wine & beer

# Shuang Cheng

☆

Shuang Cheng
Restaurant
1320 4th St. SE,
Minneapolis
378-0208

HOURS
M-Th 11-10
F,Sa 11-11

PRICES
$

CREDIT CARDS
MC/V

RESERVATIONS
Recommended

ATMOSPHERE
Very casual

ALCOHOL
Beer

Being a Chinese-food junkie actually makes me very picky about Chinese food. There are only a handful of restaurants in town that serve what I consider the genuine article, but this is one of them. The Shuang Cheng is a Chinese restaurant hybrid: It has a full dinner menu, but it also has a bit of the flavor of the little noodle houses and barbecue joints you can find in New York, Toronto or San Francisco.

From the lunch menu, the Three Delicacy combination plate offers moist and very flavorful chunks of chicken, roast pork with crackly-crisp skin, and sweet and succulent sliced cha shiu (red-glazed barbecued pork tenderloin), all piled on a mound of steamed white rice, with a garnish of crisp steamed Chinese broccoli. The lunch menu offers an assortment of other rice-plate dishes such as chicken and oyster sauce and shrimp with green peas and egg, plus such Sino-American favorites as chicken chow mein and sweet and sour pork.

The dinner menu offers heartier fare. The roast sliced duck with Chinese broccoli is flavorful shreds of duck meat tossed with slices of crisp greens. The whole lobster stir-fried in a choice of black bean sauce or ginger and scallions doesn't have a lot of meat on it, but what there is fresh, sweet and firm. The whole lobster is frequently featured as a special, for as little as $6.95. The chicken with corn-flour soup is a thick but mild blend of boneless chicken and sweet corn, large enough to serve four.

Seafood specials are frequently featured; on past visits, these have included clams with black bean sauce, and hollow vegetable with a thin and delicately flavored shrimp sauce.

# Sidney's Pizza Cafe

Sidney's has tinkered a little with the decor of the former Shelly's Woodroast, but it's basically unchanged: a rustic cabin look outside and a fireplace and lots of knotty pine inside. The big change is in the menu: While Shelly's specialized in roasted meats, Sidney's specializes in pizza and pasta; the only meat-centered choices are four rotisserie-grilled chicken entrees.

Pizza options range from barbecue chicken to Mediterranean; pasta selections include fiesta chicken (with tomatillos and mixed peppers) and rigatoni with broccoli and sun-dried tomatoes. All pastas are made on the premises. The menu designates a number of low-fat dishes.

In order to compete in Kenwood, Sidney's has to come across as something more than another mass-market pizzeria. Thus, the menu features basic fare, such as an American pizza or spaghetti with meat sauce, alongside dishes such as an Asian spicy chicken pizza and an adobe chicken rubbed with Southwestern spices (mostly chili powder, as far as I could tell).

I found Sidney's fare generally pretty good but inconsistent. Nothing was bad, but some dishes, such as the Caesar salad and the coconut chicken pasta, were too bland, while others, such as the spicy adobe chicken, were overpowering.

Among the most satisfying dishes are the goat cheese calzone, whose crisp crust sealed in the flavor and aroma of cheese, bacon, sun-dried and fresh tomatoes and garlic; and the mix of chicken and sun-dried-tomato fettuccine: The combination of those ingredients with white wine, cream and chewy house-made noodles was memorable. The apple pie pizza, topped with caramel sauce and vanilla ice cream is worth saving room for.

**Sidney's Pizza Cafe**
2120 S. Hennepin
Minneapolis
870-7000

HOURS
Su-Th 11-11
F,Sa 11-12

PRICES
$

CREDIT CARDS
AE/MC/V

RESERVATIONS
None

ATMOSPHERE
Very casual

ALCOHOL
Wine & beer

# Suzette's Cafe Exceptionale

**Suzette's Cafe Exceptionale**
498 Selby Av.
St. Paul
224-5000

HOURS
M 11-9
Tu-Th 11-10
F,Sa 11-11
Su 11-9

PRICES
$

CREDIT CARDS
AE/MC/V/CB/DC

RESERVATIONS
Recommended

ATMOSPHERE
Informal

ALCOHOL
Full bar

ENTERTAINMENT
Bands daily

OTHER
Sunday a la carte brunch

Spontaneity and improvisation are the heart of jazz, so you might expect that a jazz cafe such as Suzette's Cafe Exceptionale would create culinary compositions every night. If you write it all down, then play the same tune over and over again, the spontaneity can get lost.

The culinary score sheet at Suzette's is written down, but it shows a fair bit of improvisation. Highlights include the appetizer of cold sliced breast of roast duck stuffed with wild rice and currants, served with a tangy fresh cranberry sauce and a sweet and sharp golden mustard sauce, and the supreme of chicken with wild mushroom sauce.

In the best jazz tradition, the menu borrows a little here, a little there — the French fries with Bearnaise sauce are a signature item at Faegre's, while the spicy chicken wings with ranch dressing and celery sticks are a variation on a combo that originated at the Anchor Bar jazz club in Buffalo, N.Y.

Suzette's musical performers stay mostly in the mainstream, and the menu seems to follow the same wisdom, offering creative variations on old favorites. You can get the New York strip straight, or jazzed up with fresh peppercorns, garlic, mushrooms and a touch of brandy. The grilled salmon — a little dry but not bad — is served with a lobster sauce, while the shrimp scampi are bathed in a delicate champagne cream sauce.

The entree list also offers some dishes that you won't find on many other local menus, including the stuffed chicken legs, the Pork Diable (tenderloin finished with mushrooms and onions in a savory but mild mustard sauce) and a Mediterranean chicken — boneless breast of chicken wrapped around shrimp and spinach, served over mustard sauce. There is also short list of light (and lower priced) entrees that don't include soup or salad. The dessert offerings change daily, but the items I've sampled have been well-made.

# Swiss Alps

The former Cafe de Paris has been renamed the Swiss Alps. The menu is more-or-less classic French cuisine, which wouldn't be surprising, except that the restaurant started its life as a Haagen Dazs shop and the chef started his life in Phnomh Penh, Cambodia.

Ban Rith Yongyath escaped the killing fields of Cambodia and received his culinary training in Switzerland before coming to Minnesota. To judge by the dishes I have sampled, he's got a solid grounding in French cooking techniques. The entrees on the menu range from coquilles St. Jacques au framboise (sauteed scallops in a raspberry and wine cream sauce) and veal Wellington with shrimp stuffing, to saumon Genevoise (salmon stuffed with a duxelle of mushrooms, with a Dijon mustard shrimp sauce). A list of monthly specials offers several entrees.

The homemade desserts include a Black Forest torte and almond torte in classic style, complete with maraschino cherries, plus a choice of chocolate or caramel flan and a frozen Grand Marnier souffle with a distinct, delightful kick.

Ban Rith frequently emerges from the kitchen to greet his guests and his friendliness is one of the restaurant's attractions.

But with most of the entree prices in the expensive range (including soup or salad), this is special-occasion cuisine at special-occasion prices. The quality of the cuisine is worth the price, but the dining room lacks the amenities (such as comfortable chairs, or a wine license) that most diners expect in this price range. My inclination would be to forgo the appetizers and higher-priced entrees and stick to the lower-priced dishes.

**Swiss Alps**
701 S. Cleveland
St. Paul
690-5765

**HOURS**
Tu-Sa 11-2:30, 5:30-10
Su,M 11-2:30

**PRICES**
$$

**CREDIT CARDS**
MC/V

**RESERVATIONS**
Recommended

**ATMOSPHERE**
Informal

**ALCOHOL**
None

**OTHER**
No wheelchair access
Sunday a la carte brunch

# Table of Contents

**Table of Contents**
1648 Grand Av.
St. Paul
699-6595

**HOURS**
M-Th 7:30 a.m.-
9:30 p.m.
F 7:30-10:30
Sa 8-10:30

**PRICES**
$

**CREDIT CARDS**
None

**RESERVATIONS**
None

**ATMOSPHERE**
Informal

**ALCOHOL**
Wine & beer

**OTHER**
Small children not encouraged

I am not quite crazy enough to go into the restaurant business. But if I were, Table of Contents is the kind of place I would want to create. No tablecloths. No chandeliers. A one-page menu. Just a handful of tables and a kitchen that concentrates on doing a few things well.

The dinner menu offers just seven appetizers and four entrees: a grilled breast of chicken, grilled pork tenderloin, grilled hook-and-line-caught ocean-fish, and grilled free-range duck breast, each with a different preparation that changes nightly. That's all. Within that framework, the chef (Scot Johnson, formerly of D'Amico Cucina) manages to offer considerable variety. Nightly specials are featured, including several desserts.

I had a chance to sample a grilled breast of chicken splashed with a Balsamic vinegar and garnished with snow peas; slices of pork tenderloin finished in an orange-flavored demiglace and ringed with fresh asparagus spears; and two grilled fish preparations: salmon topped with basil and orange chunks, and firm light-fleshed spearfish.

The lunch menu offers thin-crust pizza plus an assortment of lighter fare: chicken salad with grilled grapes, basil pesto and pine nuts; a light entree of thinly sliced marinated beef on toast with red onions, tomato and arugula; a peppery homemade chicken noodle soup; and a couple of homemade pasta dishes.

The desserts show the same emphasis on simplicity: fresh strawberries laced with a caramel sauce, fresh blueberries drizzled with vanilla sauce, a simple pound cake sauteed in butter and topped with dollops of mascarpone cheese and creme Anglaise, and a dense mocha cream cake with buttercream mocha frosting and lots of coffee flavor.

# Tay Do

Tay Do is a modest cafe hidden away in the Griggs Midway building. The menu includes a section of Vietnamese specialties, ranging from seven varieties of pho, the classic beef noodle soup, to com suon bi cha, a combination plate consisting of a marinated grilled pork chop served over broken rice with shredded pork and a wedge of a Vietnamese egg cake made with ground pork, eggs and cellophane noodles.

The egg rolls are crisp and tasty, as are the chunks of deep-fried squid, but for something a little more unusual try the salad of thinly shredded green papaya with a soy-vinegar dressing, topped with thin slices of Vietnamese beef jerky and a generous quantity of fresh chopped basil. The hot and sour shrimp soup — very sour but only moderately hot — is also recommended. It's served with a generous quantity of steamed rice, to be added to the soup.

The bo nuong vi is a do-it-yourself dish. All the ingredients are delivered to your table, including thinly sliced raw beef, butter, a heaping platter of lettuce, bean sprouts, sliced cucumber, pineapple chunks, moistened sheets of rice paper and five herbs, including an Oriental basil, a mint, fresh coriander, nuoc mam fish-flavored dipping sauce and a couple of aromatic Asian greens that I was unable to identify. A little gas-fired hot plate is provided, along with a small skillet. You cook the beef in the butter to the desired degree of doneness and then roll it up along with the lettuce, herbs, cucumber, pineapple, etc. to make your own fresh spring rolls.

I was less impressed by the steamed walleye in coconut-milk sauce. The fish, which had evidently been frozen, lacked the firm but tender texture walleye has at its freshest, and the sauce added little to the dish.

**Tay Do**
1821 University
St. Paul
644-1384

**HOURS**
M-F 11-9
Sa 9-10

**PRICES**
¢

**CREDIT CARDS**
None

**ATMOSPHERE**
Very casual

**ALCOHOL**
None

# Tejas

**Tejas Restaurant**
**The Conservatory**
**800 Nicollet Mall**
**Minneapolis**
**375-0800**

**HOURS**
M-Sa 11-10

**PRICES**
$

**CREDIT CARDS**
AE/MC/V/D

**RESERVATIONS**
Recommended

**ATMOSPHERE**
Informal

**ALCOHOL**
Full bar

Tejas' rich Southwestern repertoire draws on Spanish and Indian traditions, using ingredients as diverse as pumpkin seeds, plantains, blue corn, cilantro and a wide range of chile peppers. Even the Tex-Mex staples are given imaginative twists: a grilled shrimp enchilada with smoked pepper cream and jicama relish, or barbecued duck tacos with black bean orange sauce and smoked tomato sour cream. And even humble ingredients are given the attentive and attractive presentation customary for French or California cuisine.

The most conventional of the appetizers is a platter of smoked chicken nachos with avocado salsa, Jack and Asiago cheeses and salsa roja. The more exotic choices include a masa tart with venison chili, Parmesan spoonbread and tomatilla salsa, and a wild mushroom tamale with dried fruits and sage. Equally exotic are the smoked oyster chilaquiles with cilantro pesto and Jack cheese.

Entrees range from a hot smoked beef tenderloin with guajillo whipped potatoes, barbecued corn and poblano aioli to an empanada stuffed with grilled vegetables and accompanied by a salsa verde and sweet potato chips. Tejas' answer to the fajita is a marinated, sliced flank steak, accompanied by three salsas, smoked pepper gouda and flour tortillas.

The decor is bright and colorful, the ambience cheerful and sometimes a little noisy.

# Times Bar & Cafe

The Times Bar and Cafe feels like a pub, thanks to an abundance of dark wood, little nooks and quiet corners and its air of quiet understatement. The menu is an eclectic blend of Italian, Greek and generic bistro, ranging from foccacia to steak to fondue and Brunswick stew.

The cheese fondue for two, brought to the table on a Sterno burner, is a treat. For dipping, you get a chunk of French bread and roasted potatoes; smoked ham and chopped apples are available at extra charge. The cheese isn't quite as gooey as the best homemade renditions, but it's still quite tasty.

A casserole of ravioli with marinara sauce is a bit bland, but a breast of chicken Dijon coated with chopped pecans and a mild mustard sauce is first-rate. The Times also offers a couple of meal-sized soups, including a hearty Brunswick stew made with turkey, ground sausage, corn and tomatoes. An assortment of sandwiches also is available, including burgers.

Dessert selections are limited, but include a delicious chocolate hazelnut layer cake, a very good hot apple crisp and a rich and creamy Oreo cheesecake.

---

**Times Bar & Cafe**
1036 Nicollet Mall
Minneapolis
333-2762

**HOURS**
M-Sa 11:30-1 a.m.

**PRICES**
$

**CREDIT CARDS**
AE/MC/V

**RESERVATIONS**
None

**ATMOSPHERE**
Very casual

**ALCOHOL**
Full bar

**OTHER**
Limited wheelchair access
Sunday buffet brunch

# To Chau

**To Chau**
823 University Av.
St. Paul
291-2661

HOURS
Su-F 10-9
Sa 10-10

PRICES
¢

CREDIT CARDS
None

RESERVATIONS
Recommended

ATMOSPHERE
Informal

ALCOHOL
Wine & beer

To Chau's neon sign promises Vietnamese food, but don't expect lemon grass chicken or beef with fried potatoes. To Chau's menu starts where other Vietnamese menus end.

To my taste buds, this is some of the most interesting and sophisticated food of any ethnicity to be found in the Twin Cities. Take, for example, the shrimp wrapped with beef. The modest portion of flavorful shrimp wrapped in thin sliced, broiled, marinated beef is very tasty, but it's only the beginning. Accompanying this dish is a set of do-it-yourself ingredients, including rice noodles, a stack of moistened rice paper, fresh herbs and slices of cucumber. You roll up all of the other ingredients in the rice paper and then dip into in a bowl of savory, spicy fish sauce.

Prices are ridiculously low: Nearly everything on the menu costs $6 or less. The lau thap cam is an exception, but it's ample to serve two or more. It's a bubbling Sterno-fueled hot pot, brimful with shrimp, squid, meat balls, fish cake, baby corn, carrots and Chinese cabbage in a savory broth. The banh cuon cha lua (fat rice flour noodles wrapped around a stuffing of pork, topped with slices of a mild Vietnamese bologna, slivers of fried onion and crisp vegetables) is served with a lively nuoc nam sauce for seasoning.

As with all true gastronomic adventures, satisfaction is not guaranteed. The bo kho banh mi (spicy beef stew served with French bread) is a little greasy for American tastes and the stuffed squid filled with a ground pork mix and topped with dry-fried onion is quite rubbery.

There are also some very unusual dessert drinks, all recommended, including concoctions made with longan, jackfruit and sweet green bean. The pickled plum beverage, however, is at best an acquired taste.

# Tour de France

You have to admire Scott Kee's chutzpah. Cyclist Greg LeMond of Wayzata and allergist David Morris of La Crosse, Wis., may be the principal owners of Tour de France, but chef Kee has his name plastered all over the china.

Is Kee really as good as he apparently thinks he is? Yes. Based on what I've tasted, I'd rank Tour de France on a par, gastronomically, with Goodfellow's and D'Amico Cucina. (It's also in the same price category.) The menu changes every few months, but typical fare includes an appetizer of roasted summer vegetables (eggplant, zucchini and red peppers) with white beans and grilled shrimp, duck and pesto cakes with marinated tomatoes, a salad of grilled duck breast with roasted hazelnuts and haricots verts and entrees that range from grilled chicken with corn, dumplings and tarragon cream to mustard lamb rack with mint and dried tomatoes.

Butter and cream are scarcely seen. Kee relies little on sauces, but heavily on the natural flavors of fresh, quality ingredients, enhanced with fresh herbs that can range from oregano-thyme to hyssop, lovage and pineapple sage. Rather than seduce the palate with rich, creamy sauces, Kee often challenges it with a splash of vinegar or a hint of fire. Though flavors are often robust, they are always kept in balance. Presentation is elegant and sophisticated without being fussy.

The soup and fresh fish offerings vary daily and are recommended. The desserts are very good but not quite on a par with the rest of the cuisine.

Service is prompt, attentive and extremely knowledgeable. The setting, an old Victorian house built as a church, has a simple but attractive decor, enhanced by touches of elegance such as fresh orchids at the table.

☆

Scott Kee's
Tour de France
4924 France Av. S.
Edina
929-1010

**HOURS**
T-F 11:30-9:30
Sa 5-10:30

**PRICES**
$$$

**CREDIT CARDS**
AE/MC/V

**RESERVATIONS**
Recommended

**ATMOSPHERE**
Formal

**ALCOHOL**
Wine & beer

**OTHER**
Limited wheelchair access
Limited parking
Small children not encouraged

# Tulips

**Tulips Restaurant**
452 Selby Av.
St. Paul
221-1061

**HOURS**
M-F 11:30-3
Sa,Su 5-11

**PRICES**
$

**CREDIT CARDS**
MC/V/D

**RESERVATIONS**
Recommended

**ATMOSPHERE**
Informal

**ALCOHOL**
Wine & beer

If there is such a thing as a distinctive Twin Cities restaurant style, it's the intimate bistro style exemplified by such popular Minneapolis restaurants as Lucia's, Cafe Brenda and the Loring Cafe. Tulips is the St. Paul version of that style — a little less hip, a little less sophisticated in its cuisine, a little less expensive, and a bit more neighborly in its ambience. Like the others, though, it has a spare but stylish decor and a cuisine that values freshness and simplicity over exotica.

The soups, which vary daily, may include an intense and savory cream of asparagus, a subtly nuanced lemon broccoli with chive or an underseasoned Creme de Crecy carrot soup. These were all made in the style of French potage, thickened with pureed vegetable or perhaps a little potato; I found them much more satisfying — and less caloric — than the ubiquitous high-butterfat cream soups.

The dinner menu features a few simple appetizers, including snails Bourguignonne and a well-made black olive tapenade served with French bread, and an assortment of entrees that ranges from chicken saltimbocca and a New York strip steak with sauce Bearnaise to loin pork chops with molasses and rum glaze, crepes Cordon Bleu and nightly seafood specials. These dishes are simple and rather similar in presentation, but they are quite well prepared.

The selection of desserts varies. On my visits it included a well-made but unspectacular chocolate cake, a raspberry hazelnut torte with layers of fried meringue and a rather dry Marjolaine cake.

In its pre-liquor-license days, Tulips servers were known occasionally to look the other way when patrons arrived with their own bottles. It wasn't exactly legal, but it cut down on the cost of dinner. Tulips has a license now, but the cost of drinking is still quite reasonable.

# Two Pesos

Two Pesos is an odd but successful hybrid. It's a fast-food restaurant, complete with a drive-up window and prices (on some items) that are competitive with Taco Bell across the street. But the setting is attractive enough to consider going there for a "real" dinner. It has passable inexpensive margaritas and a selection of Mexican beers. In the summertime there is an outdoor patio and the walls of the restaurant are paneled with garage-style glass doors that can be opened in good weather.

There's little on the dinner menu you haven't seen before: nachos, enchiladas, fajitas, burritos, chimichangas and chalupas (tostadas), plus soft and crispy tacos. Although the silver and china are plastic, the dishes I've sampled so far seem more nearly comparable in quality to the sit-down chains (i.e., Chi-Chi's) than to other fast-food restaurants such as Taco Bell. The beef and chicken fajita tacos are very tasty, and the borracho-style beans are cooked with pork and served in a very savory gravy. Dinner plates include rice, beans and tortillas.

The basic formula seems to be the same everywhere (plenty of chopped lettuce and tomato piled on everything), but Two Pesos adds a few nice touches. A salsa bar offers choices of mild and hot salsas and a very lively, freshly made pico de gallo sauce, plus fresh limes, onions, jalapenos and coriander. The tortillas are made on the premises — amazing for a franchised fast-food restaurant — and you can see real, whole chicken breasts being cooked on the grill for fajitas.

Two Pesos
1530 W. Lake St.
Minneapolis
825-8264

**HOURS**
M-Sa 10:30-2 a.m.
Su 10:30-midnight

**PRICES**
¢

**CREDIT CARDS**
MC/V

**RESERVATIONS**
None

**ATMOSPHERE**
Informal

**ALCOHOL**
Wine & beer

# Village Wok

**Village Wok**
610 Washington
Av. SE
Minneapolis
331-9041

HOURS
Daily
11 a.m.-2 a.m.

PRICES
$

CREDIT CARDS
AE/MC/V/DC

ATMOSPHERE
Very casual

ALCOHOL
Beer

OTHER
Limited
wheelchair access

The Village Wok is one best and most authentic of the local Cantonese restaurants.

It has a strong following among the Chinese students at the nearby University of Minnesota. That regualar clientele enables the Village Wok to bring in a good selection of fresh fish, seafood and Chinese specialty produce, which are often featured as daily specials in hand-lettered signs on the wall.

Seafood is one of the Wok's specialties. Whole Maine lobster is often featured as a special for as little as $6.95.

Other popular seafood dishes include walleye with hot meat sauce and steamed sole with black bean sauce. Be sure to try one of their hot pot dishes, such as roast pork with bean curd, chicken chunks and ginger scallions, or if you are really adventuous, duck wings and feet with black mushrooms.

Chow mein, egg foo young and other Chinese-American dishes are also available, as well as a big assortment of traditional noodle dishes and budget-priced Hong Kong rice plates.

**Money-saving tip:** The regular dinner menu is always available, but starting at 9 p.m. the restaurant also offers a late-night menu of very inexpensive noodle dishes, soups and congees (flavored rice porridges), very popular with Chinese students.

# Windows on Minnesota

As before, when this pricey and elegant eatery was the Orion Room, the strong suit at Windows on Minnesota is the view. On the 50th floor of the IDS Tower, you are seated in the clouds.

The cuisine is nouvelle hotel — a style more innovative and daring than the old hotel fare, but not quite on the cutting edge, either. For the more traditional diner, the menu offers shrimp cocktail, oysters and clams on the half-shell and Caesar salad for two, plus a typical assortment of entrees: Chateaubriand for two, steaks, lamb chops and seven kinds of fresh fish.

But there also are more imaginative offerings, including lobster ravioli with artichoke and sun-dried tomato, Maryland crab cakes with Dijon mustard sauce and a duck consomme with stuffed morels in a crust. The more interesting entrees include boneless breast of chicken stuffed with lobster, roast rack of lamb in a wild rice crust and sauteed sea scallops with cilantro butter sauce and red and black bean salad.

Overall, the quality is very good, starting with the quality of the materials.

Nearly all of the entrees are winners. The chicken stuffed with lobster is flavorful and attractively presented. The roast rack of lamb is moist and tender, its juices sealed in by the wild rice crust. Desserts also are a high point.

There are a few disappointments, particularly dishes that sound intriguing but taste ordinary. The problem seems to be instances of style triumphing over substance, such as supermarket-grade rolls served with an elegant flourish.

Then there's the matter of price. Nearly everything is a la carte, meaning you can easily spend $50 or more apiece. Add one of the more wines and you're headed for the stratosphere. Windows may well have the highest prices in the Twin Cities. But for diners who don't mind the prices — and who want something less than exotic yet still creative — Windows on Minnesota might fill the bill.

**Windows on Minnesota**
IDS Center
80 S. 8th St.
Minneapolis
349-6250

**HOURS**
M-Sa 5-midnight
Su 10:30 a.m.-3 p.m.

**PRICES**
$$$

**CREDIT CARDS**
AE/MC/V/CB/DC/D

**RESERVATIONS**
Recommended

**ATMOSPHERE**
Formal

**ALCOHOL**
Full bar

**ENTERTAINMENT**
Dancing in lounge M-Sa

**OTHER**
Sunday buffet brunch

# Yvette

**Yvette**
Riverplace
65 Main St. SE
Minneapolis
379-1111

HOURS
M 11-10
T-Th 11-11
F,Sa 11-12
Su 11-9

PRICES
$$

CREDIT CARDS
AE/MC/V/DC

RESERVATIONS
Recommended

ATMOSPHERE
Formal/informal

ALCOHOL
Full bar

ENTERTAINMENT
Music & dancing
M-Sa

OTHER
Limited
wheelchair access
Small children
not encouraged
Sunday a la carte
brunch

Yvette strives for a dual image, as restaurant and night club. The setting is strikingly romantic, with dark wood paneling and accents of gray and burgundy. It can be rather quiet early on a weeknight, but the romantic atmosphere and live music — usually mellow jazz — as well at the food, invite more diners as the evening wears on.

The cuisine emphasizes simple dishes, well prepared and attractively presented, frequently with a French accent. Typical appetizers include a shrimp scampi, prepared in a in a delicate cream sauce instead of the usual garlic butter, plus such classics as salmon gravlax, steak tartare, escargot and duck liver paté. Main course options include both a selection of lighter (and less expensive) entrees, such as a warm scallop salad, blackened New York steak or steak tartare and a regular list, which includes a grilled chicken breast in a rosemary Chardonnay wine sauce, roast duckling, sauteed sea scallops and a number of steaks and chops, as well as nightly seafood specials. I've found the cuisine to be less than exciting, but still pleasant and tasty.

Dessert offerings are minimal, but we sampled a very competent rendition of creme caramel and a tasty sweet and tart lime pie.

Service is prompt, attentive and personable.

# Short orders

## Alfaro's Mexican Restaurant
**405 E. Lake St., Minneapolis**
At Alfaro's Mexican Restaurant, the cooking is homestyle Mexican, with such familiar favorites as tamales, fajitas, enchiladas and tacos (hard or soft), plus more exotic dishes as menudo (tripe soup) and lengua (tongue). The combination plate includes your choice of three prepared meats (such as pork and cactus, beef guizado or barbacoa), with rice, beans and tortillas. The storefront cafe's homemade salsa ranks with the best in the Twin Cities. 827-1843; M-F 11-7 Sa 11-6 Su 11-4

※

## Al's Breakfast
**413 14th Av. SE., Minneapolis**
There is a slim chance of walking into Al's Breakfast and actually finding a free stool at the counter. The very narrow cafe and its 14 stools have been a Dinkytown institution for 40 years, serving up pancakes (whole wheat or buttermilk), scrambled eggs, waffles and omelettes in varieties ranging from Hawaiian (filled with chopped pork sausage and Swiss cheese and topped with sour cream and pineapple) to New Orleans (filled with shrimp, slivered almonds and capers and topped with a garlic Hollandaise.) 331-9991; M-Sa 6a.m.-1p.m. Su 9a.m.-1p.m.

※

## Annie's Parlour
**313 14th Av. SE., Minneapolis; 1827 Riverside Av., Minneapolis; Bandana Square, 1021 Bandana Blvd., St. Paul**
Classic American cuisine: burgers, malts, and french fries. You can get a plaza burger if you want (with sour cream, chives, and chopped onion on a dark bun), or a teriyaki chicken sandwich, but Annie's keeps things simple. The homestyle handcut French fries are good, but the real stars of the show are the malted milks — especially the chocolate banana. 14th Av. 379-0744, Riverside 339-6207, St. Paul 659-9138; hours vary by location

## Bayon
**724 11th Av. S., Hopkins**
Cambodian cuisine has some resemblances to Vietnamese, Thai and Chinese and some flavors all its own. You can sample them at Bayon, the Twin Cities area's only Cambodian restaurant. Specialties include curry chicken, garnish noodle and spring rolls. 935-9396; M-F 11-9 Sa,Su 4-9

※

## Bigsby's Cafe
**701 4th Av. S., Minneapolis**
   A gourmet cafeteria? The adjective is much abused, but Bigsby's Cafe probably deserves the label. Typical entrees include breast of chicken stuffed with pear, pine nuts and leeks, Argentine albondigas (meatballs) with seasoned rice, and a daily pasta offering, always made with imported pasta, plus an interesting selection of soups, salads and sandwiches, and a full bar. 338-0023; M-Su 7-8

※

## Blue Mountain Coffee House
**49 S. 9th St., Minneapolis**
   At the Blue Mountain Coffee House, you'll find Jamaican foods, T-shirts, postcards, groceries, soft drinks, and of course, Jamaican Blue Mountain Coffee. The menu includes a jerk chicken sandwich, Jamaican patties filled with beef or vegetables, and a variety of cakes, breads and coffees. 339-7156; M-F 8-7 Sa,Su 10-5

※

## Blue Nile Ethiopian Restaurant
**3008 Lyndale Av. S., Minneapolis**
   You don't need a knife and fork to eat at the Blue Nile. Most of the entrees are served with a flat, spongy sourdough bread that takes the place of cutlery — you just tear off chunks of the bread and use it as a scoop. The combination plate for two includes portions of lamb, beef, chicken and vegetable dishes, some spicy, some mild. The Blue Nile also has some dishes that you won't find at the Twin Cities' other Ethiopian restaurants, including an Ethiopian breakfast menu and several meat and vegetable dishes served over aromatic basmati rice. 823-8029; M-Th 11-10 F 11-11 Sa 9-11 Su 9-10

## Broder's Italian Cucina
**2308 W. 50th St., Minneapolis**
There are only a handful of tables at Broder's Italian Cucina, but the popular gourmet deli is a nosher's paradise. The selection of salads ranges from fusili (corkscrew noodles) with pesto and green beans to caponata, made with roasted eggplant, sweet red peppers, onions and capers; the clerks behind the counter will be happy to pile up your plate with a little bit of this and a little taste of that. And there's much more to choose from: New York style pizza, by the pie or the slice; hoagies, meats, cheeses, including homemade mascarpone cheese, breads, and a big selection of Italian desserts. 925-3113; M-F 7-9:30 Sa 8-9:30 Su 9-9:30

⚜

## Cactus Willie's
**5001 34th Av. S., Minneapolis**
Cactus Willie's, an outpost of the popular Pepito's Mexican restaurant, offers mainly nachos, burritos, tacos and the like, made with Pepito's homemade tortillas and served in generous portions at reasonable prices. The lively, fresh salsa just might be the best in town. 721-2936; M-Th 11-10 F-Su 11-11

⚜

## Cafe Latte
**850 Grand Av., St. Paul**
A gourmet cafeteria, if such a thing is possible. The daily assortment at this very popular Grand Avenue eatery always includes two stews, four soups and eight imaginative salads. The desserts are spectacular, especially the turtle cake, which has a filling of pecans, caramel and fudge oozing out between three layers of dense chocolate cake. A great place to sip a cappuccino or other coffee concoction and read the Sunday New York Times, available across the street at Odegard Books St. Paul. 224-5687; M-Th 10-11 F,Sa 9-midnight Su 9-10

## Cafe Metro
**Cargill building, 108 S. 7th St., Minneapolis**
An enthusiastic letter from a reader tipped me off to the Cafe Metro. "It has without a doubt THE BEST FOOD I've ever eaten consistently," writes Marge Youngers. "I've had absolutely wonderful soups — things like cream of celery with Stilton, Welsh leek, Canadian cheddar with stout. And the salads! Wow! ... I had a garlic linguini with fresh ginger and shrimp last week that was superb." After a couple of visits, I'm inclined to agree. It's cafeteria style and reasonably priced. **375-0668; M-F 7-3:30**

※

## Cairo Cafe
**2801 Nicollet Av. S. and 704 Hennepin Av., Minneapolis**
Think of the Cairo Cafe as the Egyptian answer to the diner. In place of meat loaf you can get either shawirma (spit-roasted seasoned pressed beef and lamb) or kibbe, a well-seasoned baked loaf of beef, lamb and cracked wheat. In addition to a hamburger served in a loaf of pita bread, the menu offers falafel, the Middle East's vegetarian answer to the slider. And if you want something more exotic than a cola, try the rania, a refreshing blend of hibiscus, tamarind and spices. There's much more, including chicken kebabs, eggplant dip, spinach pie and a delicious pot herb soup. **Nicollet 870-7871; M-Sa 11-11 Su 1-11. Hennepin 338-6810; M-Th 10:30-11 F,Sa 11-2 Su 1-11**

※

## Caravelle
**2529 Nicollet Av., Minneapolis; 799 University Av., St. Paul; 1 E. Little Canada Rd., Little Canada**
Over the years I've had some memorable meals at Caravelle. Best bets include the bo nuung ngoi (a do-it-yourself beef fondue), the lau thap cam (seafood in a hot pot) and Vietnamese lobster. Caravelle chef Tang Truong says his Vietnamese customers usually spend much less money than his non-Vietnamese customers. Non-Vietnamese customers typically order one entree per person, while the Vietnamese customers might order three entrees, and a lot of rice, to feed a family of five. **Minneapolis 871-3226, St. Paul 292-9324, Little Canada 483-1239; hours vary by location**

## Caspian Bistro
**2418 University Av. NE., Minneapolis**
The awning outside the tidy Caspian Bistro promises Greek and Mediterranean cuisine, which may puzzle students of geography, since the Caspian is an inland body of water situated between Iran and the Soviet Union. But the menu offers very tasty Persian versions of dishes that are popular throughout the Middle East, such as beef, lamb and chicken kebabs, gyros and baked eggplant, all at very reasonable prices. The adjoining grocery offers hard-to-find ingredients for Middle Eastern cooking. 623-1113; T-Th 10:30-9 F,Sa 11-10 Su 12-10

※

## Cecil's
**City Center, Minneapolis; 651 Cleveland Av. S., St. Paul**
Cecil's is the closest thing we have in the Twin Cities to a real New York-style Jewish deli, although that's not saying much. But you can get a decent corned beef or pastrami sandwich, borscht, knishes, blintzes, chicken soup with matzoh balls and most of the other staples of Jewish cookery. The front section of the establishment houses a bakery stocked with hamentaschen, bagels, challah and more, plus a small grocery store with a pretty complete selection of Jewish foods. **Minneapolis 341-0170, M-F 9-6 Sa 11-5; St. Paul 698-6276, M-Su 9-8**

※

## Cindybad Bakery and Deli
**1923 Central Av. NE., Minneapolis**
There are a couple of tables in the front of the Cindybad Bakery and Deli, and a short menu of prepared foods that includes falafel, gyros, baba ghanouj, hummus, spinach pies, meat pies and a terrific assortment of homemade pastries. The store also offers a big selection of homemade breads and imported groceries, including olives from Morocco, Turkey and Greece, feta cheese from Bulgaria, Hungary and Greece, plus coffees, spices and an assortment of items ranging from Lebanese chewing gum to canned walnuts in syrup from the Soviet Union. 788-0656; M-Sa 10:30-9 Su 12-6

## Cityscape Deli
**Lumber Exchange, 10 S. 5th St., Minneapolis**
Now it can be told: the Cityscape Deli is a CIA operation. Co-owner Peter Katsiotis is a graduate of the prestigious Culinary Institute of America in Hyde Park, New York. That may explain why you'll find the likes of shrimp gumbo, phyllo pockets stuffed with crabmeat and Brie, and stuffed mushroom caps with pesto sauce alongside the usual deli sandwiches and salads. The deli's owners roast their own meats, make their own salad dressings and bake their buns, cakes, croissants and pastries on the premises. 333-3354; M-F 6-4:30

⚜

## Cognac McCarthy's
**162 N. Dale St., St Paul**
As the name suggests, Cognac McCarthy's specializes in cognacs — 30 varieties at last count, plus a good selection of armagnacs. But there's more than just liquor: the menu offers French-Cuban chicken, grilled meatloaf, a stew du jour, mussels Miro and more, all at very reasonable prices. 224-4617; M-Sa 9-11 Su 9-9

⚜

## Coronado Foods
**197 Concord St., St. Paul**
At Coronado you can get a combination plate with two meats plus rice and beans for $4.50, or three meats for $5.50. There are no menus, but a sign on the wall lists the choices, ranging from beef fajitas and barbacoa (not spicy) to beef with chipotle peppers (spicy) and pork with chile verde sauce (very spicy). All dinners include rice and your choice of refried or spicy stewed borracho beans, plus corn or flour tortillas. 292-1988; M 11-6 T 11-4 W,Th 11-5 F 11-8 Sa 9-5 Su 9-2

## Cossetta's
**211 W. Seventh St., St. Paul**
Cossetta's may be just a cafeteria, but the simple hearty food is better — and cheaper — than you'll find at a lot of more pretentious sit-down Italian eateries around town. Typical entrees include chicken cacciatore, Italian sausage with peppers, veal Parmigiana and lasagna. But the real specialty of the house is the crisp crusty pizza, served by the slice or the pie. Adjoining the dining area is an Italian market with a very complete selection of meats, cheeses, homemade breads, imported pastas, olive oils and lots more. 222-3476; M-Sa 11-10 Su 11-8

⚜

## The Creamery
**Hwy. 25, Downsville, Wis.**

Finding a really good restaurant in the countryside is a doubly nice surprise, because such discoveries are often also bargains. The Creamery, an attractive but unpretentious inn six miles south of Menomonie, is just such a find. The restaurant's slogan is "simple food prepared with care," which describes it perfectly. The traditional American dishes are simple, such as slices of pork tenderloin topped with a fresh sage sauce, or stuffed breast of chicken with cheese and tomato sauce, but the vegetables are fresh and the kitchen makes ample use of fresh herbs in season. Other attractions include a very reasonably priced wine list and excellent desserts, including a very chocolaty German walnut cake and a homemade apple sour cream pie. The Creamery also has four rooms for nightly rental. (715) 664-8354; T-Th 11:30-2 & 5-9 F-Sa 11:30-2 & 5-10 Su 10-2 & 4:30-8

⚜

## Deco Restaurant
**Minnesota Museum of Art, 305 St. Peter St., St. Paul**

The Deco Restaurant is a hidden treasure on the fourth floor of the Minnesota Museum of Art. There's no menu; the featured lunchtime fare is an authentic Scandinavian smorgasbord, a groaning board laden with a striking display of prepared salads, fresh fruit, dessert and hot fish, pasta and meat entrees. The Sunday brunch version is even more elaborate, and somewhat more expensive. The kitchen is supervised by Soile Anderson, a well-known local chef and caterer. The Deco also is is available in the evening for private parties. 228-0520; T-F 11:30-2 Su 11-2

## Dock Cafe
**225 E. Nelson St., Stillwater**
The Dock Cafe in Stillwater is a strikingly attractive restaurant with big windows overlooking the St. Croix. The menu includes some of the usual suspects — spicy chicken wings, deep-fried calamari — plus salads and entrees of steaks, shrimp, salmon and pasta dishes and creative offerings such as a well-made chicken saltimbocca with mozzarella, provolone, prosciutto, tomatoes and basil. A more limited menu of sandwiches, salads and appetizers is served on the outdoor patio. 430-3770; M-Th 11-3:30, 5-10 F,Sa 11-3:30, 5-11 Su 10-9

## Dunn Brothers Coffee
**1569 Grand Av., St. Paul**
If you ask me, the coffee house is one of the crowning achievements of Western Civilization. In its highest form, it's not just a place to sip a cup of Java (or Sumatra Mandheling or Hawaiian Kona), but a sanctuary, a place to read books or magazines, write a journal, savor a conversation or play a friendly game of chess. Dunn Brothers offers all of this, plus the freshest cuppa money can buy. The coffee, roasted daily right on the premises, is available by the pound or by the cup (as espresso, cappuccino, mocha steamers, etc.), along with muffins and pastries from the nearby Dutch Bakery. 698-0618; M-F 7:30-11 Sa-Su 9-11

## Dupsy's African Cuisine
**474 University Av., St. Paul**
For gastronomic adventurers, Dupsy's African cuisine is a must. It is the first local restaurant to feature the cooking of West Africa. Best bets for beginners include the jollof rice (a well-seasoned dish of rice, peas, carrots and your choice of shrimp, beef or chicken) or the coconut rice (a flavorful seasoned rice dish with fish or shrimp, red pepper and coconut milk). More adventuresome souls may want to try the egusi (a stew of beef, melon seeds and greens) or the okro and stew (a delightfully slimy sauce served with meat). Both are accompanied by fufu (a starchy paste made of rice or wheat). Other recommended choices include moyin-moyin (a custard made from black-eyed peas), the oxtail pepper soup and the beef stew with rice, black-eyed peas and fresh plantains. 225-1525; M-Th 11-10 F-Su 11-11

## Edwardo's Natural Pizza
**Symphony Place, 1125 Marquette, Minneapolis; 2633 Southtown Dr., Bloomington**
Want to start a fight? Ask any two Chicagoans to name their hometown's best pizzeria. At least one of the answers is likely to be Edwardo's, famous for its stuffed deep-dish pies and now available in the Twin Cities. As the name suggests, Edwardo's puts an emphasis on quality ingredients — the basil is grown fresh right in the restaurant. The menu also offers flat pizzas, fresh pasta dishes, salads and desserts. **Minneapolis 339-9700; Su-Th 11-11 F,Sa 11-12. Bloomington 884-8400; S-Th 11-10 F,Sa 11-12**

※

## El Amenacer
**194 Concord St., St. Paul**

El Amenacer Restaurant has copied the successful Mexican formula that Coronado Foods introduced a few years ago: $4.50 buys you a heaping plate with your choice of two meat dishes, plus rice and intensely savory stewed pinto beans. The meat dishes are mostly stews, cooked long so that the meats are tender and the flavors blend together. These range from a chocolatey chicken mole with just a faint hint of sweetness, to a tart, intensely flavored beef tongue in a red chile sauce. All are spicy in the sense of being intensely seasoned, but none are particularly hot. (An excellent homemade salsa is served on the side if you want to raise the temperature.) It's all served cafeteria style, so you get to see everything before you order. 291-0758; S-Th 8-10 F,Sa 8 a.m.-3 a.m.

※

## El Meson
**3450 Lyndale Av. S., Minneapolis**

If you can't winter in the Carribbean, the next best thing might be a visit to El Meson, where at least your taste buds can take a tropical vacation. The menu features specialties from all over the Latin world, from Puerto Rican carne frita con mofongo (seasoned pork with mashed fried plantains) to arroz con pollo (chicken with seasoned rice) and the Spanish classic paella Valenciana (a big platter of yellow seasoned rice, full of shrimp, clams, mussels, lobster, squid, chicken, pork, green peas and red pimientos). 822-8062; Tu-F 11-10 Sa 12-10 Su 12-9

## Emily's Lebanese Deli
**641 University Av. NE., Minneapolis**
One of the nice things about Emily's Lebanese Deli is that it really is a deli as well as a sit-down restaurant. The cabbage rolls, stuffed grape leaves, stuffed zucchini, kibbe, hummus and baklava are behind the counter and ready to go. For little more than the cost of carryout fried chicken or burgers, you have the makings of a Middle Eastern feast that you can reheat in minutes and enjoy at home. 379-4069; M,W,Th 9-9 F,Sa 9-10

※

## Faegre's Bar and Restaurant
**430 First Av. N., Minneapolis**
Faegre's is the warehouse district's quintessential yuppie power-lunch spot. It's an attractive restaurant with a very contemporary, clean look. How's the food, you ask? Somewhat unpredictable. In the past five years, few chefs have lasted longer than six months. Some dishes have remained constant throughout the changes: the famous homemade skin-on French fries with Bearnaise sauce, the Chinese chicken salad and the Caesar salad. There are two tiers to the menu — a selection of moderately priced sandwiches and pastas and a small list of pricier beef, poultry and seafood entrees; recent selections have included a grilled eggplant sandwich, an Iowa pork chop with apple currant chutney, and penne with goat cheese and sun-dried tomato pesto. Generally the quality has been good, but entree prices have at times been higher than the level of amenities or the ambitousness of the cuisine would seem to warrant. **Money-saving tip:** Stick to the pastas, or order sandwiches and split an order of fries. 332-3515; M-Su 11:30 a.m.-12:30 a.m.

※

## Farmington Steak House
**329 3rd St., Farmington**
The steaks at the cafeteria-style Farmington Steak House are a little, shall we say, firmer than those butter-knife slabs at some fancy meat palaces, but you can't beat them for flavor. You can't beat them for price, either. Chicken, shrimp, fish and gyros dinners are also available, but skip the barbecued ribs. 463-3726; Daily 11-9

## Gallery 8
**Walker Art Center, 725 Vineland Place, Minneapolis**
You'd expect to find imaginative cuisine at an art museum, and the cafeteria at the Walker Art Center's Gallery 8 consistently delivers. The menu, which changes daily, can range from Vietnamese pork soup and Brazilian beef sandwiches to Russian cabbage borscht and a raspberry sillabub. And for the less adventuresome, there's food as simple and good as a sandwich of liverwurst and green onions, or egg salad, on homemade bread. 374-3701; T-Su 11:30-3

❧

## Gasthaus Bavarian Hunter
**8390 Lofton Av. N, Grant Township, just west of Stillwater**

Wiener schnitzel a la Holstein is one of the specialties of the house at the Gasthaus Bavarian Hunter. Feinschmeckers (gourmets) would not give passing marks to the sauerbraten or the mashed potatoes, but the schweinshaxe (pork hocks) and smoked pork chops are ausgezeichnet (excellent). Portions are generous, and the atmosphere very gemutlich (comfortable) and authentic, right down to the deer antlers on the wall and the Hacker-Pschorr on tap. 439-7128; M-Th 11-2 & 5-9 F 11-2 & 5-10 Sa 12-4 & 5-10 Su 12-8

❧

## Gasthof zur Gemutlichkeit
**W. Hwy. 12, Montrose**

Montrose, 45 miles west of Minneapolis, might seem like an unlikely location for an authentic German restaurant, but the Gasthof zur Gemutlichkeit is worth the drive. House specialties include rouladen, bratwurst, smoked pork chops, schnitzel, and the bayrische hausplatte, a feast for two that offers all of the above plus mashed potatoes, potato dumplings, spaetzle and a glass of Schinkenhager, a German firewater. 675-3777; M-Sa 11-12 Su 10:30-12

## Gingham Kitchen Cafe
**2803 43rd Av. S., Minneapolis**
Monday evenings the Gingham Kitchen Cafe serves all the lutefisk you care to eat, with meatballs, potatoes, gravy, lefse, butter and brown sugar. The restaurant wisely refuses to take sides in the cream sauce (Swedish) versus melted butter (Norwegian) controversy — it serves both. Of course, "all the lutefisk you care to eat" is a concept with different meanings to different people, particularly those who have already sampled this Nordic delicacy of lye-preserved cod. For the faint of heart, the Gingham Kitchen also serves a Monday night roast beef dinner; a full menu including steaks, chicken and breakfast items is available all day. **922-4191; M-F 6:30-8 Sa 7-8 Su 7:30-4**

## Green Mill
**57 S. Hamline, St Paul; 3626 Hennepin Av., Minneapolis; 4501 France Av., Minneapolis; 8200 Commonwealth Drive, Eden Prairie**
The menu at the Green Mill, whose original Hamline location is a popular Macalester student hangout, lists over 50 different items. But the reputation of the place is built on the deep dish pizza, which has won numerous awards over the years. The atmosphere at the various locations is casual, the kind of place you'd go for a relaxed evening out. **St. Paul 698-0353, Hennepin 374-2131, France Av. 925-5400, Eden Prairie 944-3000; hours vary by location**

## Holy Land Bakery & Deli
**2507 Central Av. NE., Minneapolis**
At the tiny Holy Land, a huge slab of spiced shawirma (gyros) meat is available in the form of a generous sandwich in a homemade pita bun, accompanied by a piece of baklava. The rest of the menu is more or less self-service: You select a mildly seasoned spinach pie or spicier vegetable pie from the cooler, and the cook will heat it for you. Also available are a smooth and garlicky hummus tahini (ground chickpea and sesame seed paste) and an irresistible baba ghanouj (roasted eggplant dip). The pita, spinach pie, vegetable pie and assorted pastries, including baklava and kataif, are made in the bakery. A big assortment of Middle Eastern groceries also is available. **781-2627; M-F 9:30-8:30 Su 10:30-3:00**

## House of Breakfast Plus
**3733 Chicago Av. S., Minneapolis**
The House of Breakfast Plus is not at all like your mom's kitchen. The Omelet Sisters, Melissa the cook and Sharon the waitress, preside over the brown and pink polka-dot emporium, and they take no guff from anyone. House rules, prominently posted, advise that patrons with bad odors or unruly children will be asked to leave. The omelets, offered in some 60 different varieties, are the specialite de la maison, but the potato pancakes are also worth a try. 823-3703; M-F 6-1 Sa 7-11

## It's Greek to Me
**626 W. Lake St., Minneapolis**
Cheap, filling and tasty Greek food in a simple but attractive setting. It's a winning combination, and it draws the big crowds that help give this popular Lake Street restaurant the noisy, crowded, boisterous feeling of a Greek taverna. All of the classics are available, from pastistio and moussaka to gyros and shish kebabs. The appetizers, including dolmades, spanikopita and saganaki, are all excellent. 825-9922; Daily 11-11

## Jerusalem's Restaurant
**1518 Nicollet Av., Minneapolis**
You'll find generous portions, reasonable prices and a good selection of Middle Eastern foods at Jerusalem's. The vegetarian combination dinner includes deep fried cauliflower, fried eggplant, potatoes, falafel and hummus served with pocket bread and salad, while the kebab combination plate delivers skewers of chicken and lamb, plus rice and salad. Belly dancers are featured Friday and Saturday nights. 871-8883; M-Su 11-11

## Joe DiMaggio Sports Bar, Pizzeria & Grill
**1298 E. Moore Lake Drive, Fridley**
Joe DiMaggio's goes beyond pizza to offer a big selection of burgers, sandwiches, salads and a couple of pasta dishes. The walls are covered with baseball murals by local artist Andy Nelson and the place has more of a family feeling than most sports bars. Worth a visit if you are in the neighborhood. 571-3417; M-Sa 11-1 Su 11-12

## Juanita's
**201 Concord St., St. Paul**
If your idea of a taco is the kind you get at Taco Bell, stuffed with ground beef and lettuce and tomatoes, you're probably not going to like Juanita's version. But if you've traveled in Mexico, and have ever tasted the flavorful little tacos stuffed with chopped beef or pork sold by the street vendors at little curbside taquerias, Juanita's tacos may bring back some happy memories. They're brought to the table with chopped onions, fresh coriander and very hot salsa that you can add to taste. The menu is limited, but several kinds of burritos are also offered. 290-2511; T-Th 11-8 F 11-10 Sa 9-2 Su 9-5

## Keys
**767 Raymond Av. and 504 N. Robert St., St. Paul; also in New Brighton, Brooklyn Park, Roseville, Crystal and White Bear Lake**
The menu at the seven Keys restaurants varies a little from place to place, but they all specialize in old-fashioned American cafe cooking, with hearty breakfasts, big burgers and such classic dinners as baked turkey and liver and onions. Portions tend toward the humongous. Raymond Av. 646-5756; Robert St. 222-4083; New Brighton 636-0662; Brooklyn Park 493-2232; Roseville 487-3530; Crystal 533-3679; White Bear Lake 426-2885; hours vary by location

## Khan's Mongolian Barbecue
**418 13th Av. SE., Minneapolis; 2720 N. Snelling Av., Roseville**

Whether or not Mongolians really cook this way, Khan's is a treat. You pick out your own raw meats (including lamb, pork, beef, turkey and chicken) plus vegetables and sauces, and then bring them to the chef, who cooks them while you watch. At lunchtime you get a single serving, including soup and appetizer; dinner includes soup, appetizer, pickled vegetables, Chinese bread and unlimited servings of the barbeque. **Minneapolis 379-3121; Roseville 631-3398; both locations M-Th 11-9:30 F 11-10 Sa 12-10 Su 5-9 (Roseville Su 12-9)**

※

## Kikugawa
**Riverplace, 43 Main St. SE, Minneapolis**

Kikugawa has managed to create an attractive Japanese ambiance, enhanced by kimonoed waitresses and traditional Japanese music. The menu offers all of the Japanese-American standards, from teriyaki steak to seafood tempura, sukiyaki, sushi and sashimi, plus a few hints of the world of Japanese cuisine that lies beyond. If you've never tried Japanese food, you can probably find a lot to enjoy at Kikugawa. Your best bet might be lunchtime, when the menu features some reasonably priced domburi offerings, traditional meal-in-a-bowl rice dishes topped with shrimp, pork or chicken. **378-3006; M-Th 11:30-2 5-10 F,Sa 11:30-11 Su 11:30-9**

※

## Kramarczuk's Eastern European Deli
**215 E. Hennepin, Minneapolis**

When it's below zero outside, and the windchill is howling up your sleeves, you don't need rabbit food; you need the kind of fare that will stick to your ribs. At Kramarczuk's, every recipe has been field-tested under Ukrainian winter conditions. It's sort of the gastronomic equivalent of putting a couple of sandbags in the your car's trunk. For example, the combination plate includes a stuffed cabbage, three varenyky (dumplings stuffed with mashed potatoes or meat) with horseradish sauce, a homemade sausage, sauerkraut and bread and butter. Also highly recommended are the borscht, Szegedin goulash, apple strudel and cheesecake. **379-3018; M-Sa 8-6**

## La Cucaracha Restaurante
**36 S. Dale St., St. Paul**
You don't have to be Mexican to cook first-rate Mexican food. At La Cucaracha, the kitchen crew has included natives of Vietnam, Laos and St. Paul, but the recipes come from the Mexican-American Flores family. Specialties of the house include homemade chicken tamales with tomatillo sauce, chicken Azteca, pollo loco (chicken with chipotle peppers in adobo sauce) and a fiesta platter (beef and chicken tacos, cheese and onion enchilada, bean tostada and Mexican rice). Prices are very reasonable, the decor is simple but attractive and the beverage choices include a nice selection of draft and imported Mexican beers, plus wines from Chile and Spain. **221-9682; Su-Th 11:30-11 F,Sa 11-1**

❀

## Leeann Chin Chinese Cuisine
**900 2nd Av. S, Minneapolis; Union Depot Place, St. Paul; 1571 S. Plymouth Rd., Minnetonka**

Leeann Chin's reputation as a cooking teacher, cookbook author and generous contributor to charitable causes has earned her a loyal following. Her formula for restaurant success is simple: familiar Chinese-American dishes such as sweet-and-sour pork, prepared with attention to quality, served in unlimited quantity (buffet-style) in strikingly attractive, even elegant surroundings. If it's authentic Cantonese cuisine you're looking for, you won't find it here, but if your taste runs more toward cream-cheese filled wontons, this might be just the ticket. Takeout kitchens are located in Bloomington, Brooklyn Center, Minneapolis, Roseville, St. Paul, Richfield and Edina. **Minneapolis 338-8488; M-Th 11-2:30 and 5-9 F,S 11-2:30 and 5-10; St. Paul 224-8814 and Minnetonka 545-3600; same hours plus Su 11-2:30**

❀

## Lee Nue Village
**866 University Av., St. Paul**

Specialties at the Twin Cities' only Hmong restaurant include fresh spring rolls, fried egg rolls and a big assortment of meal-sized noodle soups, served with beef, pork or shrimp, and accompanied by fresh bean sprouts, lime and lettuce. The adjoining video rental shop has a big selection of Thai-, Chinese-, English-, and Hindi-language videocassettes. **227-0489; M-Su 11-7**

## Le Peep
**89 S. 10th St., Minneapolis; 5500 Wayzata Blvd., Golden Valley; 444 Cedar St., St. Paul**
Le Peep may be a chain restaurant, but it really doesn't feel like one. Hanging plants and a fireplace give the place a cozy, comfortable feeling. Big breakfasts are the specialties of the house — everything from Italian sausage omelets to vegetable fritattas to eggs Benedict, pancakes and French toast. A few sandwiches are also offered for late-comers, but by early afternoon it's all over. **Minneapolis 333-1855; Golden Valley 591-5033; St. Paul 228-0805; all locations M-F 6:30-2:30 Sa,Su 7-2:30**

❀

## The Loon Cafe
**500 1st Av., N., Minneapolis**
Still a popular place with the downtown after-work crowd, this is a friendlier, mellower meat market. The menu offers award-winning chilis (including chicken), plus burgers, pork tenderloin and chicken breast sandwiches. The giant TVs are almost always tuned to sports. There's a selection of salads, soups and cold sandwiches. **332-8342; M-Sa 11 a.m.-1 a.m. Su 5-12**

❀

## Loretta's Tea Room
**2615 Park Av. S., Minneapolis**
Prices have gone up a little, but otherwise, things haven't changed much since Loretta's first opened its doors in the '30s. The tea room decor is classic Americana and so is the menu, with such specialties as chicken pot pie, walleyed pike, grilled beef tenderloin, soup and sandwich specials, salads and home-baked breads and pies. Trendier dishes such as taco salad occasionally are served as daily specials. **871-1660; M-F 11a.m.-2p.m. T,W,F 5p.m.-7:30p.m. Su 11-2**

## The Lotus
**867 Grand Av., St. Paul; 313 SE Oak St., Minneapolis; 113 W. Grant, Minneapolis; 3037 Hennepin Av., 3907 W. 50th St., Edina**
This popular chain of Vietnamese cafes relies on the same formula that has made that ethnic cuisine so popular locally: very low prices, quick service and flavorful cooking prepared with generous quantities of fresh vegetables. Unlike the Chinese chop suey-chow mein houses of a previous generation, everything is prepared to order, so vegetables are crisp and flavors distinct. St. Paul 228-9156, Oak St. 331-1781, Grant St. 870-1218, Hennepin Av. 825-2263, Edina 922-4254; hours vary by location

❦

## Lufrano's
**4257 Nicollet Av. S, Minneapolis**
Add Lufrano's to your list of good and inexpensive Italian family restaurants. The menu offers most of the familiar Italian-American favorites, such as spaghetti and meatballs, ravioli, and meatball sandwiches, plus homegrown roasted red peppers; spaghetti aglio e oglio (with olive oil, fresh garlic and anchovies); and excellent homemade pound cake and cannoli. The thin-crust pizza, available with a variety of toppings, has consistently finished near the top in local taste tests. 823-5788; M-Th 4:30-10 F,Sa 4:30-11

❦

## Lundi's Pastry
**International Plaza, 422 University Av., St. Paul**
Lundi's has the Twin Cities' largest selection of Vietnamese pastries and snacks. Items include steamed buns filled with pork, Chinese sausage, egg and pea pods; fun noodles with turkey roll, meat-filled pate chaud pastry and Vietnamese espresso filtre coffee. Other specialties include steamed sticky rice dumplings wrapped in banana leaves, asparagus crab soup, sweet sticky rice with coconut, vanilla cream puffs and traditional sweet bean drinks. 228-9217; M-Sa 11-7 Su 12-6

## Mai Village
**422 University Av., St. Paul**
The Mai Village's showpiece dish, a seven-course beef dinner called Bo 7 Mon, has more tasty Vietnamese offerings than you and several friends will be able to eat. Highlights include bo nhung dam, a do-it-yourself fondue presented with sheets of edible rice paper, fresh mint, coriander, cucumber and lettuce; and the ta pin lu thap cam, a pot of boiling broth in a tabletop cooker, served with copious quantities of beef, chicken, shrimp, pork, squid and Chinese cabbage. Other best bets include excellent eggrolls and spring rolls. 290-2585; M-Th 11-9 F 11-10 S 10-10 Su 10-9

## Market Bar-B-Que
**1414 Nicollet Av., Minneapolis; 15320 Wayzata Blvd., Minnetonka**
The original Market was demolished to make way for highway construction, but the Nicollet Av. location captures the look and spirit of the old Glenwood Av. rib joint. These are ribs for purists, served naked, with the Market's tangy sauce on the side. You can get Texas beef ribs and spareribs or a combination thereof, as well as chicken and shrimp. All come with French fries, coleslaw and white bread. Still on the barbequed theme are pork, beef, chicken and ham sandwiches touched with the spicy sauce. There are even some not-barbecued items, including an Italian sausage sandwich and a Cajun-style pork chop. Minneapolis 872-1111; M-Sa 11:30 a.m.-2:30 a.m. Su 12p.m.-1a.m.; Minnetonka 475-1770; M-S 11:30 a.m.-midnight Su 12-11

## Marquette Cafe
**Marquette Bank (10th floor), S. 6th St. and Marquette, Minneapolis**
The Marquette Cafe isn't just another employee lunchroom. It's open to the public and serves a caliber of cuisine you won't find at most cafeterias. The menu changes daily but includes soups such as shrimp and corn chowder or Spanish jambalaya, a carving station with peppered pastrami brisket one day and hickory roasted top round of beef the next, and main courses such as breast of chicken oscar or apricot-glazed pork loin stuffed with apricots and walnuts. Plus, there's an exhibition station, where chef Adam Kamerer prepares a different daily specialty, such as Santa Fe chicken pesto or Pommery shrimp in sweet mustard sauce. 341-5734; M-F 7a.m.-1:15p.m.

## The Meadows
**615 Washington Av. SE., Minneapolis**
This elegant but comfortable hotel restaurant has just a bit of the feel of a British club. The menu features wild game, with offerings ranging from shredded pheasant enchiladas with bourbon pepper sauce to New Zealand red deer with smoked tomato sauce, Manchester quails with shrimp etouffe, and Black Hills buffalo ribeye with wild mushroom ragout. Tamer fare, including tuna, salmon, lamb and several steaks, is also available. Sauces are skillfully made and presentation is a strong suit. A mixed grill offers a sampling of any three entrees with their accompanying sauces. 379-8888; M-Th 11:30-1:30, 5:30-10 F 11:30-1:30, 5:30-11 Sa 5:30-11

❧

## Milano's
**701 W. Lake St., Minneapolis**
The Sunday brunch at this inexpensive Middle Eastern/Italian restaurant includes such Middle Eastern specialties as hummus, feta cheese, olives, shawirma, rice and shakshoka (eggs with tomatoes and peppers), kofta (seasoned ground lamb) kebabs, stuffed grape leaves, eggplant salad, tabbouleh and Mediterranean pastries, plus fresh fruit, scrambled eggs, seafood pasta. Many of those same items are available a la carte on the daily lunch and dinner menu, along with an assortment of Italian and Middle Eastern entrees. Prices are very reasonable. Local musicians are featured Thursday, Friday and Saturday evenings. 827-1488; M-Su 10-11

❧

## Mud Pie
**2549 Lyndale Av. S., Minneapolis**
You can get anything you want at the Mud Pie restaurant — as long as it's vegetarian. Founded in 1972, Mud Pie still has a bit of the feel and spirit of the Woodstock/Alice's Restaurant era. The menu reflects the global variety of vegetarian cuisines: an Arabian plate of falafel, hummus, tabbouleh and tahini; spaghetti with "vegie burger" balls, Japanese vegetable tempura, Hungarian cabbage rolls, chop suey or Indian rotis, plus an extensive selection of Mexican entrees. Portions are generous, prices very reasonable, and the food tasty and filling. The menu indicates dishes made with dairy products; desserts are sweetened with honey. A good place to go for a hearty breakfast. 872-9435; M-Th 11-10 F 11-11 Sa 8 a.m.-11 p.m. Su 8 a.m.-10 p.m.

## New Riverside Cafe
**329 Cedar Av. S., Minneapolis**
The Bio-Magnetic Center of the Universe, whatever that means. In the old days, customers were invited to set their own prices and practice dishwashing yoga. Although the cafe has changed with the times, it hasn't changed that much; the spirit of the commune lives on in the worker-owned vegetarian collective. A fun place to sit on a rainy afternoon. Bean burritos, tostadas, and a vegetable stir fry are featured daily, along with sandwiches, two homemade soups and a bargain-priced plate of rice and veggies. Daily specials can range from lasagna bianca to red raga curry. The hash browns are great. Local musicians are featured Tuesday through Saturday; there is no cover charge except for special events. 333-4814; M-Th 7a.m.-11p.m. F 7a.m.-12a.m. Sa 8a.m.-12a.m. Su 9a.m.-3p.m.

※

## Nora's
**2107 E. Lake and 3118 W. Lake, Minneapolis**
It's all real at Nora's — real turkey (not processed turkey loaf), real mashed potatoes (mashed on the premises), real homemade popovers and chicken noodle soup. Just like grandma used to make, which may be why Nora's attracts a lot of seniors. And real no-nonsense waitresses who wouldn't dream of saying anything like, "Hello, my name is Kim and I'll be serving you this evening." The menu changes daily, but frequently featured items include roast pork, baked and fried chicken, spaghetti, steaks and fresh catfish, all at very reasonable prices. E. Lake 729-9353; M-Su 11-10. W. Lake 927-5781; M-Su 11-10

※

## No Wake Cafe
**100 Yacht Club Rd., St. Paul**
Real home cooking — homemade soups, muffins and pies, burgers and vegetarian sandwiches — are featured daily at the No Wake Cafe, docked just off of Harriet Island in the lower harbor of the St. Paul Yacht Club. Weekdays, the No Wake is open for breakfast and lunch. On weekends, it also features dinner specials such as barbecued ribs, walleyed pike and a vegetarian entree. The No Wake closes for the season at the end of October. 292-1411; M-F 7a.m.-2p.m. W 5-9p.m. F 5-10p.m. Sa 8-11, 12-10 Su 8-12

## Old City Cafe
**1571 Grand Av., St. Paul**
The Old City Cafe may be the Twin Cities first kosher restaurant, but you don't have to be Jewish to enjoy it — it's also one of the better vegetarian restaurants in the area. The menu features Israeli and Middle Eastern specialties such as falafel, baba ghanouj, hummus, and assorted vegetable salads plus potato kugel, New York style cheese pizza, cheesecake, baklava and cookies. **699-5347; M-Th 11:30-8:30 F 11:30-2 Su 12-8:30**

## Old Country Buffet
**Burnsville, Coon Rapids, Crystal, Fridley, Maplewood, Minnetonka, Richfield, Roseville, West St. Paul**
It's not exactly haute cuisine, but the Old Country Buffets do offer good value for the money. Next best thing to all-you-can-eat is the offering of free seconds, featured with a different menu every day of the week. Offerings can include beef barley soup, chicken and dumplings, smoked sausage and sauerkraut, fried chicken, fried cod, and Swedish meatballs, mashed potatoes, corn on the cob, a salad bar, beverages, desserts and more. **Burnsville 435-6511; Coon Rapids 421-2150; Crystal 536-8497; Fridley 572-8627; Maplewood 779-1957; Minnetonka 474-1684; Richfield 869-1240; Roseville 639-0088; West St. Paul 457-9832; hours vary by location.**

## Pacific Club
**Lumber Exchange, 10 S. 5th St., Minneapolis**
How do they do it? On weekdays and Saturdays the Pacific Club nightclub puts out a buffet spread that includes everything from pasta primavera and roast pork loin with pecan sauce over rice to peel-and-eat shrimp and beef stroganoff, plus a dazzling assortment of fresh fruits and cheeses, desserts and elegant salads. It's all free, once you pay the cover charge. Fashionable attire is required. **339-6206; M-F 4-7:30 Sa 6-8**

## Pasqual's Southwestern Deli
**2528 Hennepin Av. S., Minneapolis**

Pasqual's has a selection of Mexican foods that goes well beyond the usual local Tex-Mex offerings. In addition to first-rate burritos, enchiladas and the like, the deli case is stocked with such exotic salads as red ranch tortellini seasoned with smoky red chilis, cilantro pesto pasta salad, and black bean and corn salad with Dijon vinaigrette dressing. A small selection of hard-to-find Mexican groceries is also available. 374-1415; M-Su 10-10

※

## Peter's Grill
**114 S. 9th St., Minneapolis**

Minneapolis' oldest restaurant (founded in 1914), Peter's has moved a couple of times in recent years, but the classic art-deco furnishings have survived intact. A very popular lunch spot with the downtown crowd, Peter's specializes in classic American fare, such as roast chicken and pork chops, served by classic American waitresses. The vegetable soup and green apple pie are both excellent. The Wednesday night roast chicken dinner with all the trimmings is one of the best bargains in town. 333-1981; M-F 7 a.m.-8 p.m. Sa 8-4

※

## Pham's Vietnamese Cuisine
**Northwind Plaza, 7978 Brooklyn Blvd., Brooklyn Park**

Pham's offers an attractive decor, a selection of wines and beers and some culinary specialties that you won't find at many Vietnamese restaurants, including an appetizer of deep-fried shrimp and sweet potato. The special soup for two or more, made with pork, chicken, beef, shrimp, fish balls, bean threads and vegetables in broth, is brought to table side bubbling hot in a charcoal-burning hot pot. A word of caution: When ordering the spicy dishes, don't ask for level five (really hot) unless you really mean it. 493-2788; Su-Th 11-9 F,Sa 11-10

## Poodle Club
**3001 E. Lake St., Minneapolis**
The Poodle Club, a friendly neighborhood bar, combines festive decor with some amazing bargains. The weekend breakfast special has scrambled eggs, hash browns, ham and toast, with your choice of a screwdriver or bloody Mary, for less than $2. Wednesday evenings you can get a fried chicken dinner with wine, beer or a bar pour for only 50 cents more. The regular menu offers some good values, as well: shrimp in a basket or a rib and chicken combo. 722-1377; daily 7a.m.-1a.m.

※

## Popeye's Famous Fried Chicken & Biscuits
**732 University Av., St. Paul; 310 W. Lake St., Minneapolis**
I'm likely to lose my accreditation as a food snob in good standing for admitting this, but I actually like the gumbo and red beans and rice at Popeye's. Of all the gumbos I've sampled locally, Popeye's comes closest to the stuff I remember as a kid growing up in New Orleans. It's made with shrimp, sausage, chicken, okra, celery, tomato, and the right spices (file powder, unless I miss my guess.) I'm less wild about the fried chicken. St. Paul 293-1858; Daily 10-10. Minneapolis 825-5129; M-Sa 10:30-10, Su 11-9:30. Both locations, drive up open M-Th until 11, F,Sa until 2, Su until 10.

※

## Porky's
**1890 University Av., St. Paul**
A lot of beautifully restored hot rods and '50s vintage cruisers make the scene at Porky's, and the drive-in, a popular St. Paul hangout in the '50s and '60s, has been handsomely restored itself. The carhops are gone and the owners have added a drive-through window, but otherwise it's a pretty faithful restoration. The menu is classic drive-in fare: burgers, fries, fried chicken, first-rate onion rings and fresh strawberry pie. 644-1790; Su-Th 11-11 Fri-Sa 11-12

## Porter's Bar & Grill
**2647 Nicollet Av. S., Minneapolis**
Porter's makes the effort to be more than just another neighborhood saloon. Among the little extra touches are a well-seasoned homemade chili, plus steaks, burgers and an assortment of sandwiches and munchies. The decor of beer memorabilia is augmented by a nice selection of beer imports. Porter's also encourages a responsible approach to drinking: Parties of three or more can pick a "designated driver" who gets free soft drinks all night. 872-0808; M-Sa 11:30-1 a.m. Su 11-1 p.m.

※

## Poulet
**2558 Lyndale Av. S., Minneapolis**
There's more than just poulet at Poulet. Imaginative chicken dishes such as Peking poulet and Punjab poulet are the specialty of the house, but an assortment of seafood dishes have been added to the menu. New items include salmon St. Jean, poulet promenade and poulet spinach salad. 871-6631; M-F 7-10 Sa 7:30-10 Su 8-4

※

## Quang Pastry and Deli
**2734 Nicollet Av. S., Minneapolis**
This tiny storefront cafe serves very tasty Vietnamese snack foods. Specialties of the house include grilled marinated pork with broken-grain rice, coconut sweet rice dessert, rice cakes, a steamed meat-filled bun, a pork sandwich, fresh spring rolls, and five kinds of dessert drinks, flavored with everything from coconut and seaweed to dried plums and black-eyed peas and mung beans. An assortment of meal-sized soups is also available. 870-4739; M,W-Su 10-9

## Red Sea
**320 Cedar Av. S., Minneapolis**
At the Red Sea, one of a trio of Ethiopian restaurants in the Cedar-Riverside neighborhood, the menu features a choice of spicy or mild lamb, chicken, beef and vegetarian dishes, all reasonably priced. Most are served on top of the traditional Ethiopian flat bread, which also takes the place of silverware — you simply tear off pieces of the bread and scoop up meat and veggies. Also recommended is the foule Sudanese style, a spicy African version of refried beans. 333-1644; daily 11-1

## Rick's Ol' Time Cafe
**3756 Grand Av., Minneapolis**
From the outside, Rick's Ol' Time Cafe looks like an overgrown summer cabin, but inside, you'll find some surprises. In addition to the usual breakfast items and sandwiches, Rick's offers some very tasty and uncommon specialties, including wild rice pancakes and Colombian-style (scrambled) huevos rancheros. 827-8948; M-F 6:30-3 Sa 7:30-3 Su 8-2

## Rosewood Room
**Omni Northstar Hotel, 618 2nd Av. S., Minneapolis**
There was a time when the Rosewood Room ranked second only to the legendary Charlie's Cafe in the pantheon of Twin Cities gastronomy. But to judge by a recent visit, the Rosewood Room has quietly decided to withdraw from the crowded competition for the gourmet dollar. The current menu offers "no-surprises" fare for the hotel clientele. But if you aren't really a picky eater and are looking for an elegant atmosphere without the fancy sauces and weird vegetables of high cuisine, the Rosewood Room may fit the bill. The rosewood decor is as charming as ever and the service staff, including several waitresses with many years of experience, does a fine job. 333-2313; M 7 a.m.-2 p.m. T-Th 7 a.m.-2 p.m., 6-10 F,Sa 7-2, 6-10:30 Su 7 a.m.-11 a.m.

## Ruby's Cafe
**1614 Harmon Pl., Minneapolis**
Hearty breakfasts, such as the Ruby's special (scrambled eggs with veggies and cheese) and the Zorbett Omelette (made with black olives, spinach and feta cheese), are the specialties of the house at Ruby's Cafe, alongside Loring Park in Minneapolis. Breakfasts, served all day, include hash browns or home fries and a choice of buttermilk biscuit, muffin or toast. Sandwiches and burgers are available from 10:30 a.m. till closing. **338-2089; M-F 7-3 Sa 7-2 Su 8-2**

※

## Rudolph's Bar-B-Que
**1933 Lyndale Av. S., Minneapolis; 366 Jackson St., St. Paul**

Rudolph's still doesn't get a lot of respect from local rib fans, but a few years back, these guys won a couple of national barbecue cook-off contests. The restaurants have a movie motif, with lots of publicity stills and dinner specials with names like Mr. Moto (a half-slab of ribs) and the Rhett Butler (2 pieces of Texas beef rib and half a spring chicken). **Minneapolis 871-8969, M-Sa 11-2 Su 10-12; St. Paul 222-2226 M-Th 11-11 F,S 11-1 a.m. Su 4-10**

※

## Russian Piroshki and Tea House
**1758 University Av., St. Paul**

At the tiny Russian Piroshki and Tea House you can get Russian-style home cooking, ready made to carry out. The specialties of the house include baked and fried piroshkis (the Russian answer to the hamburger), beet borscht, stuffed cabbage and tea cakes. Seating is very limited, and so are the hours. **646-4144; T-F 11-6**

## Russian Village
**248 Cleveland Av., St. Paul**
The Russian Village market and delicatessen carries a full line of Eastern European specialties, ranging from borscht and smoked fish to Siberian pirmeny (meat dumplings), homemade vareneki (cheese- and potato-filled dumplings) and desserts. You can even take a sausage tour of Russia and Eastern Europe: there are four varieties of Ukrainian kielbasa, two Russian bolognas and a raft of sausages named after cities (instead of frankfurters or weiners, try a tube steak named after Odessa, Moscow, Lwow, Warsaw, Minsk, Kiev or Krakow). The Russian Village isn't a restaurant, but there are a couple of tables in the front of the store, and sandwiches and soups are available to eat there. 699-6330; M 11-5 T-Sa 10-8 Su 11-5

## Sahari
**1831 Nicollet Av. S, Minneapolis**
There are a few Greek dishes on the Sahari's menu, such as moussaka and a Greek salad, but most of the offerings are traditional Arabic specialties such as kebabs of beef, chicken or seasoned ground beef and lamb, and kubbeh (deep-fried patties of cracked wheat, stuffed with ground lamb, beef and pine nuts). Vegetarian dishes are a strong suit at Sahari — in addition to very tasty falafel (seasoned deep-fried chick-pea patties), foule madamas (a garlicky fava bean dip) and hummus (a dip made of garbanzo beans and sesame paste), the menu offers mojedara (a savory dish of seasoned rice and lentils). If you have room for dessert, the rolle nut (a tube of phyllo pastry filled with walnuts, butter and cinnamon), the baklava and the halvah (sweetened ground sesame seeds with pistachios) all are recommended. 870-0071; M-Sa 11-10 Su 5-10

## St. Martin's Table
**2001 Riverside Av., Minneapolis**
The servers are all volunteers at this vegetarian cafe, operated by the community of St. Martin, an ecumenical Christian community commited to the cause of peace. All of their tips are donated to a charitable cause involved in feeding the hungry or working for social justice (a different cause is selected each month). The menu is a simple one of vegetarian soups, sandwiches and desserts, all made from scratch. 339-3920; M-Sa 9:30-5

## Sasha's Deli and Grill
**Minnetonka Boat Works, 294 E. Grove Ln., Wayzata**
Now that Sasha's isn't pretending to be a real deli anymore, I like it a lot better. Lox and cream cheese, matzo ball soup, and deli sandwiches are still offered, but the rest of the menu runs the gamut from grilled chicken satay to shrimp with lemon garlic pasta and daily fish specials, all with a nice view of Wayzata Bay. 475-3354; M-Th 11-10 F 11-11 Sa 8-11 Su 8-10

※

## Scandia Bakery & Konditori
**2713 E. Lake St., Minneapolis**
The classic German Konditorei is a gilded palace of gastronomic sin, where well-fed burghers drink coffee from china cups and eat fancy pastries topped with lots of schlag (whipped cream). The Scandinavian version, as presented at the Scandia Bakery & Konditori is a more restrained and sensible affair. You pour your own coffee, the cups are plastic and the desserts aren't really sinful. They're still delicious, though — Danish kringler and almond kransakake and fyrste kake with a few Bohemian kolacky thrown in for ethnic diversity. 724-5411; M-F 6-5:30 Su 8-Noon

※

## 700 Express
**Dayton's Minneapolis, 700 Nicollet Mall**
The last time I was in Paris, cafes were offering, in place of the multicourse lunch, a simple cold plate made up of a slice or two of dried saucisson, a little homemade pate, a wedge of farm cheese and a slice or two of rustic country bread, all to be washed down with a glass of simple red wine. The Marketplace Sampler offered at 700 Express, the fast-service cafe in Dayton's 700 Under the Mall, is a pretty good imitation. The sampler varies from week to week, but when I tried it, it included a few slices of roast beef, a little garlic sausage, some French Morbiers cheese and a fresh-baked roll. I can also recommend the hearty black bean soup and the nutty wild rice cake. 375-2684; M-F 11-8:30 Sa 11-5 Su 12-5

## Seward Community Cafe
**2129 E. Franklin Av., Minneapolis**
You fill out your own order and bus your own dishes at the "worker managed, community-owned" Seward Community Cafe. Famous for its hearty earth breakfasts and homemade hash browns, the Seward also offers burgers (beef or vegetarian) and weekly specials that run the gamut from chicken cacciatore to tofu stroganoff, all at very reasonable prices. 332-1011; T 7-11:30p.m. M,W-F 7-9 p.m. Sa,Su 8-9

⚜

## Signature Cafe
**130 Warwick St. SE., Minneapolis**
Tucked away on a shady residential street, the Signature Cafe has everything a neighborhood eatery should offer: good food, very reasonable prices and a very congenial atmosphere. It features Middle Eastern appetizers and salad, plus sandwiches, freshly made pastas, nightly fresh fish specials and more. 378-0237; M 11-2p.m. T-Sa 11-9

⚜

## SkyRoom
**Dayton's Minneapolis, 700 Nicollet Mall**
If you can't find anything you want to eat at Dayton's SkyRoom restaurant, you're just too picky. The 12th-floor lunchroom in the downtown Minneapolis store is five restaurants in one: a 40-foot-long salad bar, a pizza bar, a deli counter, the Chickery, which specializes in char-broiled chicken, and Grill It, which offers grilled fish, grilled pork, beef and chicken kebabs and grilled burgers. The view of the downtown skyline is striking, and the piano player in white tie and tails is a nice touch. 375-4559; M-Sa 11-3

## Smoke House
**500 E. Lake St., Minneapolis**
Several testimonials from Minnesota Vikings football players are posted at the counter at the Smoke House, attesting to the quality of the little carry-out's ribs. The football players evidently appreciate quantity as well as quality; the slabs of ribs that the Smoke House sells are meaty, tender and big. Both mild and hot sauces are available; if you order the hot sauce, get it on the side. (Don't say I didn't warn you.) 824-0558; M-Th 11-11 Fri,Sa 11-2a.m. Su 12-8

❈

## Sri Lanka Curry House
**2821 Hennepin Av. S., Minneapolis**
There is a secret to enjoying the hot and spicy food at the Sri Lanka Curry House: You have to leave your machismo (or machisma) behind. Swaggering types who walk in with the I-can-take-it-as-hot-as-you-can-dish-it-out attitude frequently walk out with the gastrointestinal equivalent of third-degree burns. Midwestern taste buds generally aren't conditioned to handle the spicy Ceylonese curries and rotis at full strength. So stick to mild or medium, at least the first time around. And if you do overdo it (or even if you don't), cool off with a cold and creamy passionfruit shake. 871-2400; M-W 5-10 Th 11:30-10 F 11:30-11 Sa 1-11 Su 4:30-10

❈

## Studio Restaurant
**2400 3rd Av. S., Minneapolis**
In a setting as inspiring as the Minneapolis Institute of Arts, you can expect the cooks at the Studio Restaurant to come up with creative offerings for their lunchtime cafeteria menu. Offerings can range from Thai-style noodles with pork and shrimp to Chicken Creole, polenta with roasted vegetables and salade Nicoise. 870-3180; T-Su 11-2:30

## Suzume
**3814 W. 51st St., Edina**
Oyako domburi (a rice dish topped with chicken and egg) is just one of the traditional Japanese menu items at Suzume. Other enjoyable dishes include the shrimp tempura, tekka-maki (tuna) sushi and nabeyaki udon, a soup made with udon noodles. **927-6559; M-F 5-9 Sa 5-10 Su 5-10**

❊

## Szechuan Express
**2650 Hennepin Av., Minneapolis; 9818 Aldrich Av. S, Bloomington**

For about the price of a big burger and fries, you can get an order of Kung Pao chicken with fried rice or pork with hot garlic sauce at the Szechuan Express. And nearly as fast: My order of half a dozen different dishes was cooked to order and delivered at the drive-up window in less than 10 minutes. The Szechuan dishes are available in degrees of hotness that range from hot to devastating, but there are plenty of milder choices as well. **Minneapolis 374-1535 M-Su 11-10; Bloomington 881-8068 M-S 11-10 Su 4-10**

❊

## Taj Mahal Groceries and Restaurant
**Rice Creek Shopping Center, 2134B Silver Lake Rd., New Brighton**

The Taj Mahal, arguably the smallest restaurant in the Twin Cities, has one table and six chairs; I highly recommend the takeout alternative. The menu, which changes every few days, consists of about four items — a biryani (the Indian version of fried rice), a curry (usually chicken), a vegetable dish and a potato curry or a dish made from potato and eggplant. The best time to visit is probably on Friday evenings and Saturdays, when masala dosa is also on the menu. Dosas are a specialty of southern India, a thin, very large pancake made from a batter of rice and lentil flours and fried on a hot griddle. A masala dosa is served stuffed with a very flavorful but not overpoweringly spicy potato curry. **636-0719; T-F 12-8 Sa,Su 10-5**

## Tandoor Restaurant
**210 E. Hennepin Av., Minneapolis**
Specialties of the house, prepared in an authentic clay tandoor oven, include tandoor chicken, chicken tikka (skewered boneless marinated chicken), seikh kebab (skewers of minced lamb) and authentic nan breads. A variety of vegetarian dishes is also available. 378-2055; M-F 11:30-2 & 5:30-9 Sa 5:30-9

※

## Ted Cook's 19th Hole
**2814 E. 38th St., Minneapolis**
Do you have trouble getting ribs to turn out right on the backyard grill? Here's an easy, foolproof method. Start the fire in your grill. About half an hour before you're ready to eat, jump into the car and drive over to Ted Cook's to and pick up a slab of meaty, flavorful spare ribs. Just before you're ready to eat, toss the ribs on the grill, and invite your friends and neighbors. No one need ever be any the wiser. 721-2023; T-Th 11-12 Fri 11-1 Sa 1-1 Su 1-10

※

## Thanh Quan
**2725 University Av. SE., Minneapolis**
Thanh Quan serves very fine Vietnamese cuisine at very reasonable prices. The menu offers some specialties few other Vietnamese restaurants offer, most notably a sweet and sour (and spicy) shrimp soup called canh chua tom. Served in a very large bowl, this medley of shrimp, tomatoes, noodles, cracklings, celery, spices, holy basil and broth is large enough to make a meal for two. A more elaborate version of this dish is the lau thap cam (a charcoal-burning hot pot filled with shrimp, pork, chicken, squid, crab and vegetables) served only after 4 p.m. 378-1255; M-Th 11-9 F 11-10 Sa 12-10 Su 12-9

## Toulouse
**Gaviidae Commons, 651 Nicollet Mall, Minneapolis**
Toulouse, the lunch spot on the fifth floor of Gaviidae Common in downtown Minneapolis, serves fresh and flavorful food with a southern French accent, ranging from grilled chicken with couscous and currants to a Toulouse pizza topped with roasted leeks, tomatoes, mozzarella and goat cheese, plus an assortment of salads, sandwiches and tempting desserts. 342-2700; M-Sa 11-2:30 & 5:30-10

⁂

## Trieu Chau Village
**500 University Av., St. Paul**
At Trieu Chau Village, a modest storefront, the usual selection of Vietnamese dishes is augmented by a back-page list called "Vietnamese specialties." Most of these are meal-in-a-bowl dishes: flavorful broths brimming with egg noodles or rice noodles, garnished with roast duck or barbecued pork or beef, or combinations of shrimp and pork and squid. Among them are eight different versions of pho, the national dish of Vietnam. Pho consists of thinly sliced beef in a clear broth with rice noodles, onions and bean sprouts, with fresh bean sprouts, herbs and a wedge of lime served as accompaniments. 222-6148; Su-Th 10-10 F,Sa 10-2 a.m.

⁂

## Trout-Air Restaurant
**14536 West Freeway Drive, Forest Lake**
It doesn't get any fresher than this: at Trout-Air you can catch your own trout, in indoor or outdoor ponds, and then either take it home or have it prepared the way you like — broiled or deep-fried. Tackle is provided and no license is necessary. Or you can just order from the menu, which also offers smoked trout, steak and seafood. 464-2964; M-Su 11:30-9

## Trung Nam French Bakery
**Minnehaha Mall, 767 N. Milton, St. Paul**
The French colonial occupation of Vietnam ended in 1954, but the French influence on Vietnamese cooking can still be seen at the Trung Nam French Bakery, where you'll find croissants, baguettes, sweet rolls and filtered coffee side by side with Vietnamese steamed buns, soups and iced drinks. Or try a Franco-Vietnamese hybrid — Vietnamese barbecued pork with fresh cilantro, a Vietnamese version of French pate, cucumber and sliced carrot and chili pepper stuffed in a French baguette. Trung Nam also serves a short list of Vietnamese soups. 488-6449; M-Sa 7:30-6 Su 7:30-10

## Wienery
**414 Cedar Av. S., Minneapolis**
For real Chicago-style hot dogs head for the Wienery, on the West Bank in Minneapolis. The Wienery specializes in Vienna brand beef hot dogs, available Chicago style, Warsaw style, Manhattan style, Mexicali style or plain. Burgers, chicken sandwiches, Italian beef and falafel also are available. 333-5798; M-Sa 11-8

## Yangtze
**5625 Wayzata Blvd., St. Louis Park**
The Chinese perfected snacking and grazing centuries ago when they invented dim sum, the assortment of Chinese snacks. You order as few or as many as you like and when you're finished the waiter counts up the empty dishes. The Yangtze offers an unusually good selection on Sundays, ranging from shrimp dumplings and meat balls to squid, duck feet and riblets in black bean sauce. 541-9469; M-Th 11-10 Fri 11-11 Sa 10-11 Su 10-10

# Indexes & maps

# INDEX BY CUISINE
## Afghan

| | |
|---|---|
| Caravan Serai ......................... 21 | Khyber Pass ............................ 60 |
| Da Afghan .............................. 30 | |

## American

| | |
|---|---|
| Afton House Inn ........................ 9 | Loretta's Tea Room ............. 139 |
| Annie's Parlour ..................... 123 | Lowell Inn .............................. 70 |
| Creamery ............................... 129 | Market Bar-B-Que ............... 141 |
| Dakota Bar & Grill ................. 31 | Meadows ............................... 142 |
| Dixie's Bar & Smokehouse Grill ...................................... 34 | Minnesota Zephyr ................. 77 |
| Dock Cafe .............................. 130 | Nicollet Island Inn ................ 85 |
| Dover Restaurant & Bar ........ 35 | Nora's ................................... 143 |
| Gingham Kitchen Cafe ........ 134 | No Wake Cafe ...................... 143 |
| Harbor View Cafe ................... 48 | Nye's Polonaise Room .......... 87 |
| Heartthrob Cafe ..................... 50 | Old Country Buffet .............. 144 |
| Jax ........................................... 53 | Peter's Grill .......................... 145 |
| J.D. Hoyt's .............................. 54 | Poodle Club .......................... 146 |
| Jenning's Red Coach Inn ....... 55 | Popeye's Famous Fried Chicken ............................. 146 |
| Joe DiMaggio's Sports Bar, Pizzeria & Grill ................ 136 | Porky's .................................. 146 |
| Joe Senser's Sports Grill & Bar ....................................... 57 | Porter's Bar & Grill .............. 147 |
| Jose's American Grill ............. 58 | Rudolph's Bar-B-Que .......... 149 |
| Keys ....................................... 136 | St. Paul Grill .......................... 99 |
| Kincaid's Steak, Chop & Fish House ................................... 61 | Smoke House ....................... 153 |
| Lexington ................................ 67 | Ted Cook's 19th Hole .......... 155 |
| Loon Cafe ............................. 139 | Trout-Air Restaurant ........... 156 |
| | Whitney Grille |
| | Wienery ................................ 157 |
| | Windows on Minnesota ....... 119 |

## Breakfast

| | |
|---|---|
| Al's Breakfast ....................... 123 | Le Peep ................................. 139 |
| House of Breakfast Plus ...... 135 | Ruby's Cafe .......................... 149 |
| Keys ....................................... 136 | |

## British

| | |
|---|---|
| Brit's Pub & Eating Establishment ..................... 18 | Corby's on the Croix ............. 29 |
| | Sherlock's Home .................. 104 |

# Index

## Cajun/Creole

Dixie's Bar & Smokehouse Grill..................34
Emporium of Jazz..................37
J.D. Hoyt's..................54
Popeye's Famous Fried Chicken..................146

## Cambodian

Bayon..................124

## Caribbean

Chez Bananas..................22
Harry Singh's Caribbean..................49

## Chinese

Beijing..................14
Far East..................39
Jien Fung..................56
Keefer Court..................59
Khan's Mongolian Barbecue..................137
Leeann Chin..................138
My Le Hoa..................81
Nankin..................82
Rainbow Chinese Restaurant..................94
Shuang Cheng..................106
Szechuan Express..................154
Village Wok..................118
Yangtze..................157

## Coffee Houses

Blue Mountain Coffee House..................124
Dunn Brothers Coffee..................130

## Continental

Corby's on the Croix..................29
510 Restaurant..................42
Forepaugh's..................43
Latour..................64
Le Carrousel..................66
Rosewood Room..................148
Windows on Minnesota..................119

## Deli

Broder's Italian Cucina..................125
Cecil's Delicatessen..................127
Cindybad Bakery & Deli..................127
Cityscape Deli..................128
Emily's Lebanese Deli..................132
Holy Land Bakery & Deli..................134

## Deli (continued)

Kramarczuk's Eastern European Deli.................137
Pasqual's Southwestern Deli.......................145
Quang Pastry & Deli............147
Russian Village......................150
Sasha's Deli & Grill...............151

## Eastern European

Kramarczuk's Eastern European Deli....................137
Nye's Polonaise Room...........87

## Eclectic

Azur....................................12
Bigsby's Cafe........................124
Dakota Bar & Grill.................31
Cafe Brenda..............................19
Cafe Latte.............................125
Cafe Metro.............................126
Chez Bananas........................22
Cognac McCarthy's...............128
Duggan's................................36
Faegre's.................................132
Figlio.....................................40
Gallery 8...............................133
Goodfellow's..........................46
Living Room..........................68
Loring Cafe............................69
Lowry's...................................71
Lucia's....................................72
Marquette Cafe.....................141
Muffuletta in the Park...........79
New French Cafe...................83
Nikki's...................................86
Pacific Club...........................144
Pickled Parrot........................90
Poulet....................................147
Rick's Ol' Time Cafe............148
Sasha's Deli & Grill..............151
Scully's..................................103
700 Express..........................151
Sidney's Pizza Cafe.............107
Signature Cafe......................152
SkyRoom................................152
Studio Restaurant................153
Suzette's Cafe Exceptionale 108
Table of Contents.................110
Times Bar & Cafe.................113
Toulouse...............................156
Yvette...................................120

## Ethiopian

Blue Nile..............................124
Odaa......................................88
Red Sea...............................148

## Fish & Seafood

Anthony's Wharf ..................... 10
Blue Point ............................... 16
Emporium of Jazz .................. 37
Fitzgerald's ............................. 41
Kincaid's Steak, Chop & Fish
    House ................................. 61
Newport SeaGrill .................... 84

## French

Azur ........................................ 12
Chez Colette ........................... 23
Chez Daniel ............................ 24
Chez Paul ............................... 25
Corby's on the Croix .............. 29
Forepaugh's ............................ 43
Le Cafe Royale ....................... 65
New French Cafe .................... 83
Quail on the Hill .................... 93
Swiss Alps ............................ 109
Toulouse ............................... 156
Tour de France ..................... 115
Tulips ................................... 116

## German

Black Forest Inn ..................... 15
Gasthaus Bavarian Hunter .. 133
Gasthof zur Gemutlichkeit .. 133

## Greek

Acropol Inn ............................... 8
Christos .................................. 26
It's Greek to Me .................... 135
Sahari ................................... 150

## Hmong

Lee Nue Village .................... 138

## Indian

Delites of India ...................... 33
Fair Oaks Hotel &
    Restaurant ......................... 38
Taj Mahal Groceries &
    Restaurant ....................... 154
Tandoor Restaurant ............. 155

## Italian

| | |
|---|---|
| Bocce ................................. 17 | Gustino's ........................... 47 |
| Broder's Italian Cucina ........ 125 | Lowry's .............................. 71 |
| Cafe di Napoli ..................... 20 | Lufrano's ......................... 140 |
| Ciatti's ............................... 27 | Mama D's .......................... 73 |
| Coco Lezzone ...................... 28 | Mama Mia's ....................... 74 |
| Cossetta's ......................... 129 | Polo Italia .......................... 91 |
| D'Amico Cucina ................... 32 | Pronto Ristorante ............... 92 |
| Edwardo's Natural Pizza ..... 131 | Ristorante Luci ................... 95 |
| Giorgio's ............................. 44 | Rossini's Trattoria .............. 96 |
| Green Mill ......................... 134 | |

## Japanese

| | |
|---|---|
| Ichiban ............................... 51 | Sakura ............................. 100 |
| Kikugawa ......................... 137 | Samurai Steak House ........ 101 |
| Origami .............................. 89 | Suzume ............................ 154 |

## Korean

| | |
|---|---|
| Mirror of Korea .................... 78 | Shilla Stone BBQ ............... 105 |

## Latin American

| | |
|---|---|
| El Meson .......................... 131 | La Corvina ......................... 62 |

## Mexican

| | |
|---|---|
| Acapulco Bar & Grill ............... 7 | Jose's American Grill ........... 58 |
| Alfaro's Mexican | La Corvina ......................... 62 |
| Restaurant ..................... 123 | La Cucaracha ................... 138 |
| Cactus Willie's .................. 125 | Pasqual's Southwestern |
| Coronado Foods ................. 128 | Deli ................................ 145 |
| El Amenacer ..................... 131 | Tejas ............................... 112 |
| Juanita's .......................... 136 | Two Pesos ........................ 117 |

## Middle Eastern

| | |
|---|---|
| Cairo Cafe ........................ 126 | Emily's Lebanese Deli ......... 132 |
| Caspian Bistro .................. 127 | Holy Land Bakery & Deli .... 134 |
| Cindybad Bakery & Deli ...... 127 | Jacob's 101 Lounge ............. 52 |

## Middle Eastern (continued)

Jerusalem's ................ 135
Milano's ..................... 142
Old City Cafe ............. 144
Sahari ......................... 150
Signature Cafe ........... 152

## Moroccan

Barbary Fig .................. 13

## Pizza

Edwardo's Natural Pizza ..... 131
Green Mill ........................... 134
Joe DiMaggio's Sports Bar,
  Pizzeria & Grill ................ 136
Nikki's ................................... 86
Sidney's Pizza Cafe ............ 107

## Russian

Russian Piroshki & Tea House ............ 149
Russian Village ............ 150

## Scandinavian

Deco Restaurant ............... 129
Gingham Kitchen Cafe ..... 134
Scandia Bakery & Konditori ............ 151

## Self-Service

Bigsby's Cafe ..................... 124
Cafe Latte ......................... 125
Coronado Foods ................ 128
Cossetta's ......................... 129
Gallery 8 ........................... 133
Khan's Mongolian Barbecue ............ 137
Leeann Chin ..................... 138
Marquette Cafe ................. 141
New Riverside Cafe .......... 143
Pacific Club ...................... 144
Pasqual's Southwestern Deli ............ 145
Popeye's Famous Fried Chicken ....... 146
Seward Community Cafe ..... 152
SkyRoom ............................... 152
Studio Restaurant ............... 153
Szechuan Express ................ 154
Toulouse .............................. 156
Two Pesos ............................ 117

## Steak

Austin's Steak House ............. 11
Farmington Steak House ...... 132
Ichiban ....................................... 51
J.D. Hoyt's ............................... 54
Kincaid's Steak, Chop & Fish House ..................................... 61
Mancini's ................................. 75
Manny's Steakhouse ............... 76
Murray's Restaurant & Lounge .................................. 80
Samurai Steak House ............ 101

## Sri Lankan

Sri Lanka Curry House ......... 153

## Thai

Royal Orchid ........................... 97
Ruam Mit Thai ....................... 98
Sawatdee ............................... 102

## Vegetarian/Natural food

Cafe Brenda ............................ 19
Delites of India ....................... 33
Good Earth .............................. 45
Mud Pie ................................. 142
New Riverside Cafe .............. 143
Old City Cafe ........................ 144
St. Martin's Table ................ 150
Seward Community Cafe ..... 152

## Vietnamese

Caravelle .............................. 126
Lan Xang ................................ 63
Lotus ..................................... 140
Lundi's Pastry ...................... 140
Mai Village ........................... 141
Pham's Vietnamese Cuisine 145
Quang Pastry & Deli ............ 147
Tay Do .................................. 111
Thanh Quan .......................... 155
To Chau ................................ 114
Trieu Chau Village ............... 156
Trung Nam French Bakery . 157

## West African

Dupsy's African Cuisine ...... 130

## INDEX BY PRICE

The price categories, based on a typical dinner (when available), not including beverage and tip:

| | | |
|---|---|---|
| ¢ | Inexpensive | Less than $10 per person |
| $ | Moderate | $10 to $19 per person |
| $$ | Expensive | $20 to $29 per person |
| $$$ | Very expensive | $30 or more per person |

## ¢ Inexpensive

Alfaro's Mexican Restaurant .......................... 123
Al's Breakfast ....................... 123
Annie's Parlour ..................... 123
Blue Mountain Coffee House ................................ 124
Broder's Italian Cucina ........ 125
Cactus Willie's ...................... 125
Cafe di Napoli ......................... 20
Cafe Latte ............................. 125
Cafe Metro ............................ 126
Cairo Cafe ............................. 126
Caravelle ............................... 126
Caspian Bistro ..................... 127
Cecil's Delicatessen ............. 127
Cindybad Bakery & Deli ...... 127
Cityscape Deli ...................... 128
Coronado Foods .................... 128
Cossetta's ............................. 129
Deco Restaurant ................... 129
Dunn Brothers Coffee ........... 130
Dupsy's African Cuisine ...... 130
Edwardo's Natural Pizza ..... 131
El Amenacer .......................... 131
Emily's Lebanese Deli .......... 132
Emporium of Jazz .................. 37
Fair Oaks Hotel & Restaurant .......................... 38
Farmington Steak House ..... 132
Gallery 8 ............................... 133
Gingham Kitchen Cafe ........ 134
Green Mill ............................. 134
Harry Singh's Caribbean ...... 49
Holy Land Bakery & Deli .... 134
House of Breakfast Plus ...... 135
It's Greek to Me .................... 135
Jerusalem's ........................... 135
Juanita's ............................... 136
Keefer Court ........................... 59
Keys ...................................... 136
Kramarczuk's Eastern European Deli .................. 137
Lan Xang ................................ 63
Le Peep ................................. 139
Lee Nue Village .................... 138
Loon Cafe .............................. 139
Loretta's Tea Room .............. 139
Lotus .................................... 140
Lufrano's .............................. 140
Lundi's Pastry ...................... 140
Mai Village ........................... 141
Marquette Cafe .................... 141
Mud Pie ................................ 142
New Riverside Cafe .............. 143
Nora's ................................... 143
No Wake Cafe ....................... 143
Old City Cafe ........................ 144
Old Country Buffet .............. 144
Pacific Club .......................... 144
Pasqual's Southwestern Deli .................................... 145
Pham's Vietnamese Cuisine 145
Poodle Club .......................... 146
Popeye's Famous Fried Chicken ............................. 146
Porky's ................................. 146
Quang Pastry & Deli ............ 147
Red Sea ................................ 148

## ¢ Inexpensive (continued)

Rick's Ol' Time Cafe ............ 148
Ruby's Cafe ........................ 149
Russian Piroshki & Tea House ............................. 149
Russian Village ..................... 150
Sahari ................................ 150
St. Martin's Table ................ 150
Scandia Bakery & Konditori ......................... 151
Seward Community Cafe ..... 152
SkyRoom ............................ 152
Smoke House ...................... 153
Studio Restaurant ................ 153
Szechuan Express ................ 154
Taj Mahal Groceries & Restaurant ........................ 154
Tandoor Restaurant ............. 155
Tay Do ................................ 111
Ted Cook's 19th Hole .......... 155
Thanh Quan ........................ 155
To Chau .............................. 114
Toulouse ............................. 156
Trieu Chau Village ............... 156
Trung Nam French Bakery . 157
Two Pesos ........................... 117
Wienery .............................. 157

## $ Moderate

Acapulco Bar & Grill ............... 7
Acropol Inn ............................ 8
Barbary Fig ......................... 13
Bayon ................................ 124
Beijing ................................ 14
Bigsby's Cafe ..................... 124
Black Forest Inn .................. 15
Blue Nile ........................... 124
Bocce ................................. 17
Brit's Pub & Eating Establishment ..................... 18
Caffe Pronto ....................... 92
Caravan Serai ..................... 21
Chez Bananas ..................... 22
Chez Paul (cafe) .................. 25
Christos .............................. 26
Ciatti's ................................ 27
Cognac McCarthy's ............ 128
Creamery .......................... 129
Da Afghan .......................... 30
Delites of India ................... 33
Dock Cafe ......................... 130
Dover Restaurant & Bar ........ 35
Duggan's ............................ 36
El Meson ........................... 131
Faegre's ............................ 132
Far East ............................. 39
Figlio .................................. 40
Fitzgerald's ......................... 41
Gasthaus Bavarian Hunter .. 133
Gasthof zur Gemutlichkeit .. 133
Giorgio's ............................. 44
Good Earth ......................... 45
Harbor View Cafe ................ 48
Heartthrob Cafe .................. 50
Ichiban ............................... 51
Jacob's 101 Lounge ............. 52
Jenning's Red Coach Inn ....... 55
Jien Fung ............................ 56
Joe DiMaggio's Sports Bar, Pizzeria & Grill ................ 136
Joe Senser's Sports Grill & Bar ................................. 57
Jose's American Grill ........... 58
Khan's Mongolian Barbecue ........................ 137
Khyber Pass ........................ 60
Kikugawa .......................... 137
La Corvina .......................... 62
La Cucaracha .................... 138
Leeann Chin ...................... 138
Living Room ....................... 68
Lowry's .............................. 71
Mama D's ........................... 73

# Index

## $ Moderate (continued)

Mama Mia's ............................... 74
Mancini's .................................. 75
Market Bar-B-Que ................ 141
Milano's ................................. 142
Mirror of Korea ....................... 78
Muffuletta in the Park ............ 79
My Le Hoa .............................. 81
Nankin ................................... 82
Nikki's .................................... 86
Nye's Polonaise Room ............ 87
Odaa ....................................... 88
Peter's Grill .......................... 145
Pickled Parrot ......................... 90
Polo Italia ............................... 91
Porter's Bar & Grill .............. 147
Poulet ................................... 147
Rainbow Chinese Restaurant 94
Ristorante Luci ....................... 95
Rossini's Trattoria .................. 96
Royal Orchid .......................... 97
Ruam Mit Thai ....................... 98

Rudolph's Bar-B-Que .......... 149
Sakura .................................. 100
Samurai Steak House .......... 101
Sasha's Deli & Grill ............. 151
Sawatdee .............................. 102
Scully's ................................. 103
700 Express ......................... 151
Shilla Stone BBQ ................ 105
Shuang Cheng ..................... 106
Sidney's Pizza Cafe ............. 107
Signature Cafe ..................... 152
Sri Lanka Curry House ....... 153
Suzette's Cafe Exceptionale 108
Suzume ................................ 154
Table of Contents ................ 110
Tejas .................................... 112
Times Bar & Cafe ................ 113
Trout-Air Restaurant ........... 156
Tulips ................................... 116
Village Wok ......................... 118
Yangtze ................................ 157

## $$ Expensive

Afton House Inn ...................... 9
Anthony's Wharf ................... 10
Austin's Steak House ............. 11
Blue Point .............................. 16
Cafe Brenda ........................... 19
Chez Colette .......................... 23
Chez Daniel ........................... 24
Chez Paul ............................... 25
Coco Lezzone ........................ 28
Corby's on the Croix ............. 29
Dakota Bar & Grill ................ 31
Dixie's Bar & Smokehouse
   Grill ................................... 34
Forepaugh's ........................... 43
Jax ......................................... 53
J.D. Hoyt's ............................. 54
Kincaid's Steak, Chop & Fish
   House ................................ 61

Le Carrousel .......................... 66
Lexington .............................. 67
Loring Cafe ........................... 69
Lowell Inn ............................. 70
Lucia's ................................... 72
Meadows .............................. 142
Newport SeaGrill ................... 84
Nicollet Island Inn ................. 85
Origami .................................. 89
Pronto Ristorante ................... 92
Quail on the Hill .................... 93
Rosewood Room .................. 148
St. Paul Grill .......................... 99
Sherlock's Home .................. 104
Swiss Alps ........................... 109
Yvette .................................. 120

## $$$ Very expensive

| | |
|---|---|
| Azur ........................................12 | Manny's Steakhouse ..............76 |
| D'Amico Gucina .....................32 | Minnesota Zephyr ...................77 |
| 510 Restaurant ......................42 | Murray's Restaurant & |
| Goodfellow's............................46 | Lounge ................................80 |
| Gustino's .................................47 | New French Cafe....................83 |
| Latour......................................64 | Tour de France .....................115 |
| Le Cafe Royale........................65 | Windows on Minnesota.......119 |

## Jeremy's favorite restaurants

☆ ☆

| | |
|---|---|
| Azur ........................................12 | Mirror of Korea......................78 |
| Barbary Fig.............................13 | My Le Hoa..............................81 |
| Black Forest Inn.....................15 | Odaa........................................88 |
| Cafe Brenda ...........................19 | Pronto Ristorante ..................92 |
| Coco Lezzone..........................28 | Rainbow Chinese Restaurant 94 |
| Dakota Bar & Grill.................31 | Ristorante Luci.......................95 |
| D'Amico Cucina .....................32 | Royal Orchid...........................97 |
| Delites of India ......................33 | Ruam Mit Thai ......................98 |
| Far East...................................39 | Sherlock's Home...................104 |
| Goodfellow's............................46 | Shuang Cheng.......................106 |
| Harbor View Cafe...................48 | Table of Contents..................110 |
| Khyber Pass............................60 | To Chau.................................114 |
| Living Room ...........................68 | Tour de France .....................115 |
| Lucia's.....................................72 | Village Wok...........................118 |

# Index

## Sunday brunch

Afton House Inn ........................ 9
Beijing ...................................... 14
Bocce ........................................ 17
Chez Colette ............................ 23
Chez Daniel ............................. 24
Chez Paul ................................. 25
Ciatti's ..................................... 27
Corby's on the Croix ............... 29
Creamery ............................... 129
Dakota Bar & Grill ................. 31
Deco Restaurant ................... 129
Delites of India ....................... 33
Dixie's Bar & Smokehouse
  Grill ...................................... 34
Dover Restaurant & Bar ........ 35
Duggan's .................................. 36
Faegre's ................................. 132
Far East ................................... 39
Figlio ........................................ 40
Fitzgerald's ............................. 41
Gasthaus Bavarian Hunter .. 133
Gasthof zur Gemutlichkeit .. 133
Jacob's 101 Lounge ................. 52
Jax ............................................ 53
J.D. Hoyt's ............................... 54
Jien Fung ................................. 56

Kincaid's Steak, Chop & Fish
  House .................................... 61
Latour ...................................... 64
Lexington ................................ 67
Loretta's Tea Room .............. 139
Lowry's .................................... 71
Lucia's ..................................... 72
Milano's ................................. 142
Muffuletta in the Park .......... 79
My Le Hoa ............................... 81
Nankin ..................................... 82
New French Cafe .................... 83
New Riverside Cafe ............. 143
Newport SeaGrill .................... 84
Nicollet Island Inn ................. 85
Nikki's ..................................... 86
Rudolph's Bar-B-Que .......... 149
Sasha's Deli & Grill ............. 151
Sawatdee ............................... 102
Scully's .................................. 103
Signature Cafe ...................... 152
Suzette's Cafe Exceptionale 108
Table of Contents ................. 110
Times Bar & Cafe ................. 113
Windows on Minnesota ....... 119
Yvette ................................... 120

## Rooms with a view

Anthony's Wharf ..................... 10
Dock Cafe .............................. 130
Fitzgerald's ............................. 41
Le Carrousel ........................... 66
Minnesota Zephyr ................... 77

Newport SeaGrill .................... 84
Nicollet Island Inn ................. 85
No Wake Cafe ....................... 143
SkyRoom ............................... 152
Windows on Minnesota ....... 119

## Outdoor dining

Anthony's Wharf ..................10
Barbary Fig .........................13
Black Forest Inn ...................15
Blue Point ...........................16
Chez Paul ............................25
Ciatti's ................................27
Dakota Bar & Grill ................31
Dock Cafe ..........................130
Faegre's .............................132
Figlio ...................................40
Gallery 8 ............................133
Giorgio's ..............................44
Jax ......................................53
Jerusalem's ........................135
Jose's American Grill ............58
Kramarczuk's Eastern
    European Deli ................137
Loring Cafe ..........................69
Lucia's .................................72
Mud Pie .............................142
Muffuletta in the Park ..........79
Newport SeaGrill ..................84
Nicollet Island Inn ................85
Nikki's .................................86
Pasqual's Southwestern
    Deli ...............................145
Poulet ................................147
Ruby's Cafe .......................149
Seward Community Cafe .....152
Sidney's Pizza Cafe .............107
Signature Cafe ....................152
Suzette's Cafe Exceptionale 108
Tejas ..................................112
Two Pesos ..........................117
Yvette ................................120

## Good with kids

Alfaro's Mexican
    Restaurant .....................123
Annie's Parlour ...................123
Cafe Brenda .........................19
Emily's Lebanese Deli ..........132
Good Earth ..........................45
Harbor View Cafe .................48
Heartthrob Cafe ...................50
Lan Xang .............................63
Leeann Chin .......................138
Lee Nue Village ..................138
Lotus .................................140
Lufrano's ...........................140
Lundi's Pastry ....................140
Mai Village ........................141
Mama D's ............................73
Mirror of Korea ....................78
Mud Pie .............................142
My Le Hoa ...........................81
Nankin ................................82
Nora's ................................143
Odaa ...................................88
Old Country Buffet .............144
Pham's Vietnamese Cuisine 145
Popeye's Famous Fried
    Chicken .........................146
Rainbow Chinese Restaurant 94
Royal Orchid ........................97
Seward Community Cafe .....152
Shuang Cheng ....................106
Sidney's Pizza Cafe .............107
SkyRoom ...........................152
Szechuan Express ...............154
Tay Do ...............................111
Thanh Quan .......................155
To Chau .............................114
Trieu Chau Village ..............156
Trung Nam French Bakery .157
Two Pesos ..........................117
Village Wok .......................118

## Late-night dining (after 11 p.m.)

| | |
|---|---|
| Acapulco Bar & Grill................7 | Loring Cafe .............................69 |
| Bocce ........................................17 | Market Bar-B-Que ...............141 |
| Cafe di Napoli........................20 | New French Cafe....................83 |
| Cafe Latte .............................125 | New Riverside Cafe.............143 |
| Chez Bananas ........................22 | Nye's Polonaise Room..........87 |
| Coco Lezzone..........................28 | Origami....................................89 |
| Dixie's Bar & Smokehouse Grill.....................................34 | Pickled Parrot........................90 |
| Edwardo's Natural Pizza.....131 | Poodle Club..........................146 |
| El Amenacer..........................131 | Porky's...................................146 |
| Faegre's..................................132 | Porter's Bar & Grill.............147 |
| Gasthof zur Gemutlichkeit..133 | Rainbow Chinese Restaurant 94 |
| Giorgio's ..................................44 | Red Sea.................................148 |
| Heartthrob Cafe .....................50 | Ruby's Cafe ..........................149 |
| Joe DiMaggio's Sports Bar, Pizzeria & Grill..................136 | Rudolph's Bar-B-Que ..........149 |
| | Scully's ..................................103 |
| Joe Senser's Sports Grill & Bar........................................57 | Sidney's Pizza Cafe.............107 |
| | Smoke House.......................153 |
| Jose's American Grill.............58 | Ted Cook's 19th Hole .........155 |
| La Cucaracha........................138 | Times Bar & Cafe................113 |
| Le Carrousel...........................66 | Trieu Chau Village ..............156 |
| Lexington ................................67 | Two Pesos.............................117 |
| Living Room ...........................68 | Village Wok..........................118 |
| Loon Cafe..............................139 | Windows on Minnesota.......119 |

## Romantic dining

| | |
|---|---|
| Afton House Inn......................9 | Le Cafe Royale.......................65 |
| Azur.........................................12 | Le Carrousel...........................66 |
| Barbary Fig.............................13 | Living Room ...........................68 |
| Cafe Brenda ...........................19 | Loring Cafe .............................69 |
| Cafe Latte .............................125 | Lowry's....................................71 |
| Chez Bananas ........................22 | Lucia's.....................................72 |
| Dakota Bar & Grill.................31 | Meadows................................142 |
| D'Amico Cucina .....................32 | New French Cafe....................83 |
| Deco Restaurant...................129 | Pronto Ristorante ..................92 |
| 510 Restaurant .......................42 | Quail on the Hill....................93 |
| Giorgio's..................................44 | Rosewood Room ...................148 |
| Goodfellow's...........................46 | Tour de France .....................115 |
| Gustino's.................................47 | Windows on Minnesota.......119 |
| Kikugawa..............................137 | Yvette....................................120 |
| Latour......................................64 | |

## INDEX BY LOCATION
### East suburbs

Afton House Inn .......................... 9
Ciatti's ...................................... 27
Corby's on the Croix ................ 29
Creamery ................................ 129
Dock Cafe ............................... 130
Emporium of Jazz .................... 37
Gasthaus Bavarian Hunter .. 133
Jose's American Grill ............. 58
Keys ........................................ 136
Lowell Inn ................................ 70
Minnesota Zephyr ................... 77
Old Country Buffet ............... 144

### Minneapolis downtown

510 Restaurant ........................ 42
700 Express ........................... 151
Acapulco Bar & Grill ................. 7
Annie's Parlour ...................... 123
Anthony's Wharf ..................... 10
Azur .......................................... 12
Bigsby's Cafe ......................... 124
Blue Mountain Coffee
  House .................................. 124
Bocce ....................................... 17
Brit's Pub & Eating
  Establishment ...................... 18
Cafe Brenda ............................. 19
Cafe di Napoli .......................... 20
Cafe Metro ............................. 126
Cairo Cafe .............................. 126
Cecil's Delicatessen ............... 127
Chez Bananas .......................... 22
Chez Paul ................................. 25
Ciatti's ...................................... 27
Cityscape Deli ........................ 128
D'Amico Cucina ....................... 32
Edwardo's Natural Pizza ..... 131
Faegre's ................................. 132
Goodfellow's ............................ 46
Gustino's .................................. 47
Ichiban ..................................... 51
J.D. Hoyt's ............................... 54
Jerusalem's ............................ 135
Jose's American Grill ............. 58
Keefer Court ........................... 59
Kikugawa ............................... 137
Leeann Chin .......................... 138
Le Peep .................................. 139
Living Room ............................ 68
Loon Cafe ............................... 139
Loring Cafe ............................. 69
Lotus ...................................... 140
Mama Mia's ............................. 74
Manny's Steakhouse .............. 76
Market Bar-B-Que ................ 141
Marquette Cafe ..................... 141
Murray's Restaurant &
  Lounge ................................. 80
Nankin ..................................... 82
New French Cafe .................... 83
Newport SeaGrill .................... 84
New Riverside Cafe .............. 143
Nicollet Island Inn .................. 85
Nikki's ...................................... 86
Odaa ........................................ 88
Origami .................................... 89
Pacific Club ........................... 144
Peter's Grill ........................... 145
Pickled Parrot ......................... 90
Pronto Ristorante ................... 92
Red Sea ................................. 148
Rosewood Room ................... 148
Royal Orchid ........................... 97
Ruby's Cafe ........................... 149
Sawatdee ............................... 102
SkyRoom ............................... 152
Tejas ...................................... 112
Times Bar & Cafe ................. 113
Toulouse ................................ 156
Wienery ................................. 157
Windows on Minnesota ....... 119
Yvette .................................... 120

## Minneapolis north and east

| | |
|---|---|
| Al's Breakfast .........................123 | Lan Xang ...............................63 |
| Annie's Parlour......................123 | Lotus....................................140 |
| Caspian Bistro ......................127 | Meadows..............................142 |
| Cindybad Bakery & Deli......127 | Nye's Polonaise Room ...........87 |
| Emily's Lebanese Deli..........132 | Shuang Cheng......................106 |
| Holy Land Bakery & Deli....134 | Signature Cafe .....................152 |
| Jacob's 101 Lounge .................52 | Tandoor Restaurant.............155 |
| Jax...........................................53 | Thanh Quan.........................155 |
| Khan's Mongolian Barbecue...........................137 | Village Wok..........................118 |
| Kramarczuk's Eastern European Deli ...................137 | |

## Minneapolis south and west

| | |
|---|---|
| Alfaro's Mexican Restaurant.........................123 | House of Breakfast Plus ......135 |
| Broder's Italian Cucina........125 | Loretta's Tea Room .............139 |
| Cactus Willie's ......................125 | Lufrano's...............................140 |
| Christos..................................26 | Mirror of Korea .....................78 |
| El Meson ...............................131 | Nora's...................................143 |
| Fair Oaks Hotel & Restaurant...........................38 | Poodle Club..........................146 |
| Far East..................................39 | Rick's Ol' Time Cafe............148 |
| Gingham Kitchen Cafe........134 | Scandia Bakery & Konditori..........................151 |
| Green Mill............................134 | Seward Community Cafe.....152 |
| | Ted Cook's 19th Hole ..........155 |

## Minneapolis Uptown

| | |
|---|---|
| Annie's Parlour......................123 | Lotus....................................140 |
| Black Forest Inn.....................15 | Lowry's...................................71 |
| Blue Nile ..............................124 | Lucia's...................................72 |
| Cairo Cafe ............................126 | Milano's................................142 |
| Caravelle...............................126 | Mud Pie................................142 |
| Delites of India ......................33 | Pasqual's Southwestern Deli ...................................145 |
| Figlio......................................40 | Popeye's Famous Fried Chicken ...........................146 |
| Gallery 8...............................133 | Porter's Bar & Grill..............147 |
| Giorgio's.................................44 | Poulet ...................................147 |
| Good Earth ............................45 | Quang Pastry & Deli ...........147 |
| Green Mill............................134 | Rainbow Chinese Restaurant 94 |
| Harry Singh's Caribbean .......49 | |
| It's Greek to Me...................135 | |

## Minneapolis Uptown (continued)

Rudolph's Bar-B-Que .......... 149
Sahari ...................... 150
Sidney's Pizza Cafe .......... 107
Smoke House .................. 153
Sri Lanka Curry House ........ 153
Studio Restaurant ............ 153
Szechuan Express ............. 154
Two Pesos .................... 117

## North suburbs

Ciatti's ...................... 27
Good Earth .................... 45
Joe DiMaggio's Sports Bar, Pizzeria & Grill ............ 136
Joe Senser's Sports Grill & Bar .......................... 57
Keys ......................... 136
Khan's Mongolian Barbecue .................... 137
Mama D's ...................... 73
My Le Hoa ..................... 81
Old Country Buffet ........... 144
Pham's Vietnamese Cuisine 145
Taj Mahal Groceries & Restaurant ................. 154
Trout-Air Restaurant ......... 156

## St. Paul downtown and east

Coronado Foods ............... 128
Cossetta's ................... 129
Deco Restaurant .............. 129
El Amenacer .................. 131
Fitzgerald's .................. 41
Forepaugh's ................... 43
Heartthrob Cafe ............... 50
Juanita's .................... 136
Keys ......................... 136
Le Carrousel .................. 66
Leeann Chin .................. 138
Le Peep ...................... 139
No Wake Cafe ................. 143
Ruam Mit Thai ................. 98
Rudolph's Bar-B-Que .......... 149
St. Martin's Table ........... 150
St. Paul Grill ................ 99
Sakura ....................... 100
Sawatdee ..................... 102

## St. Paul west

Acropol Inn .................... 8
Barbary Fig ................... 13
Cafe Latte ................... 125
Caravan Serai ................. 21
Cecil's Delicatessen ......... 127
Ciatti's ...................... 27
Cognac McCarthy's ............ 128
Dakota Bar & Grill ............ 31
Dixie's Bar & Smokehouse Grill ....................... 34
Dunn Brothers Coffee ......... 130
Dupsy's African Cuisine ...... 130
Green Mill ................... 134
Jose's American Grill ......... 58
Khyber Pass ................... 60
La Corvina .................... 62

## St. Paul west (continued)

La Cucaracha .......................... 138
Lee Nue Village ...................... 138
Lexington ................................. 67
Lotus ....................................... 140
Lundi's Pastry ....................... 140
Mai Village ............................. 141
Mama D's ................................. 73
Mancini's ................................. 75
Muffuletta in the Park ........... 79
Old City Cafe ........................ 144
Popeye's Famous Fried
 Chicken ............................. 146
Porky's ................................... 146
Quail on the Hill ..................... 93
Ristorante Luci ........................ 95
Russian Piroshki & Tea
 House ................................ 149
Russian Village ..................... 150
Shilla Stone BBQ ................. 105
Suzette's Cafe Exceptionale 108
Swiss Alps ............................. 109
Table of Contents ................. 110
Tay Do .................................... 111
To Chau ................................. 114
Trieu Chau Village ............... 156
Trung Nam French Bakery . 157
Tulips .................................... 116

## South suburbs

Chez Colette ............................ 23
Chez Daniel ............................. 24
Ciatti's ..................................... 27
Da Afghan ............................... 30
Farmington Steak House ..... 132
Good Earth ............................. 45
Harbor View Cafe ................... 48
Joe Senser's Sports Grill &
 Bar ....................................... 57
Kincaid's Steak, Chop & Fish
 House ................................... 61
Latour ...................................... 64
Le Cafe Royale ........................ 65
Lotus ...................................... 140
Old Country Buffet .............. 144
Rossini's Trattoria ................. 96
Sawatdee ............................... 102
Scully's .................................. 103
Suzume .................................. 154
Szechuan Express ................. 154
Tour de France ..................... 115

## West suburbs

Austin's Steak House ............. 11
Bayon .................................... 124
Beijing ..................................... 14
Blue Point ............................... 16
Ciatti's ..................................... 27
Coco Lezzone .......................... 28
Dover Restaurant & Bar ........ 35
Duggan's ................................. 36
Gasthof zur Gemutlichkeit .. 133
Green Mill ............................. 134
Jenning's Red Coach Inn ....... 55
Jien Fung ................................ 56
Leeann Chin ......................... 138
Le Peep .................................. 139
Market Bar-B-Que ............... 141
Old Country Buffet .............. 144
Polo Italia ............................... 91
Samurai Steak House ........... 101
Sasha's Deli & Grill ............. 151
Sherlock's Home ................... 104
Yangtze ................................. 157

# Map of Minneapolis Area

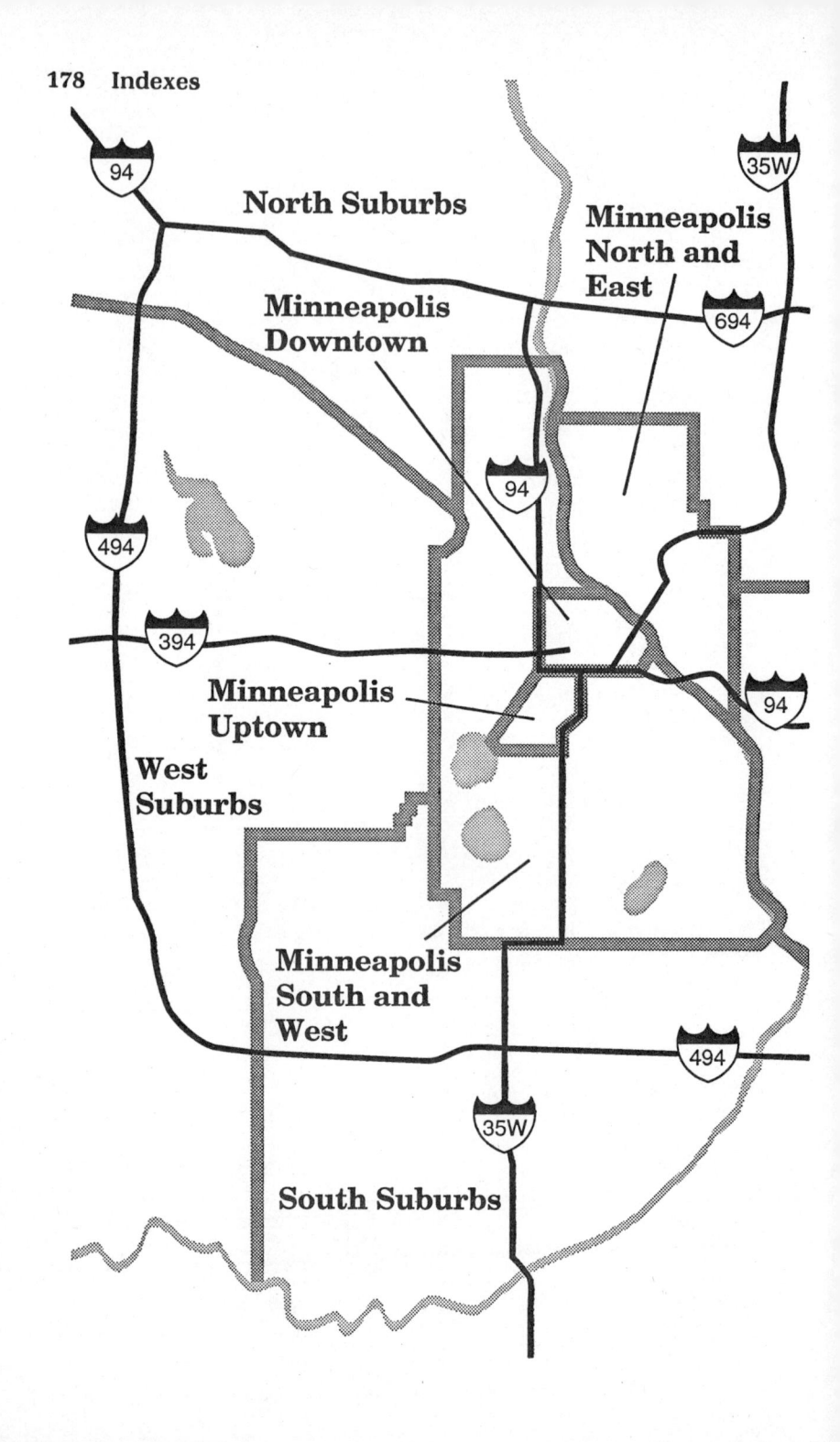

- North Suburbs
- Minneapolis North and East
- Minneapolis Downtown
- Minneapolis Uptown
- West Suburbs
- Minneapolis South and West
- South Suburbs

# Indexes 179

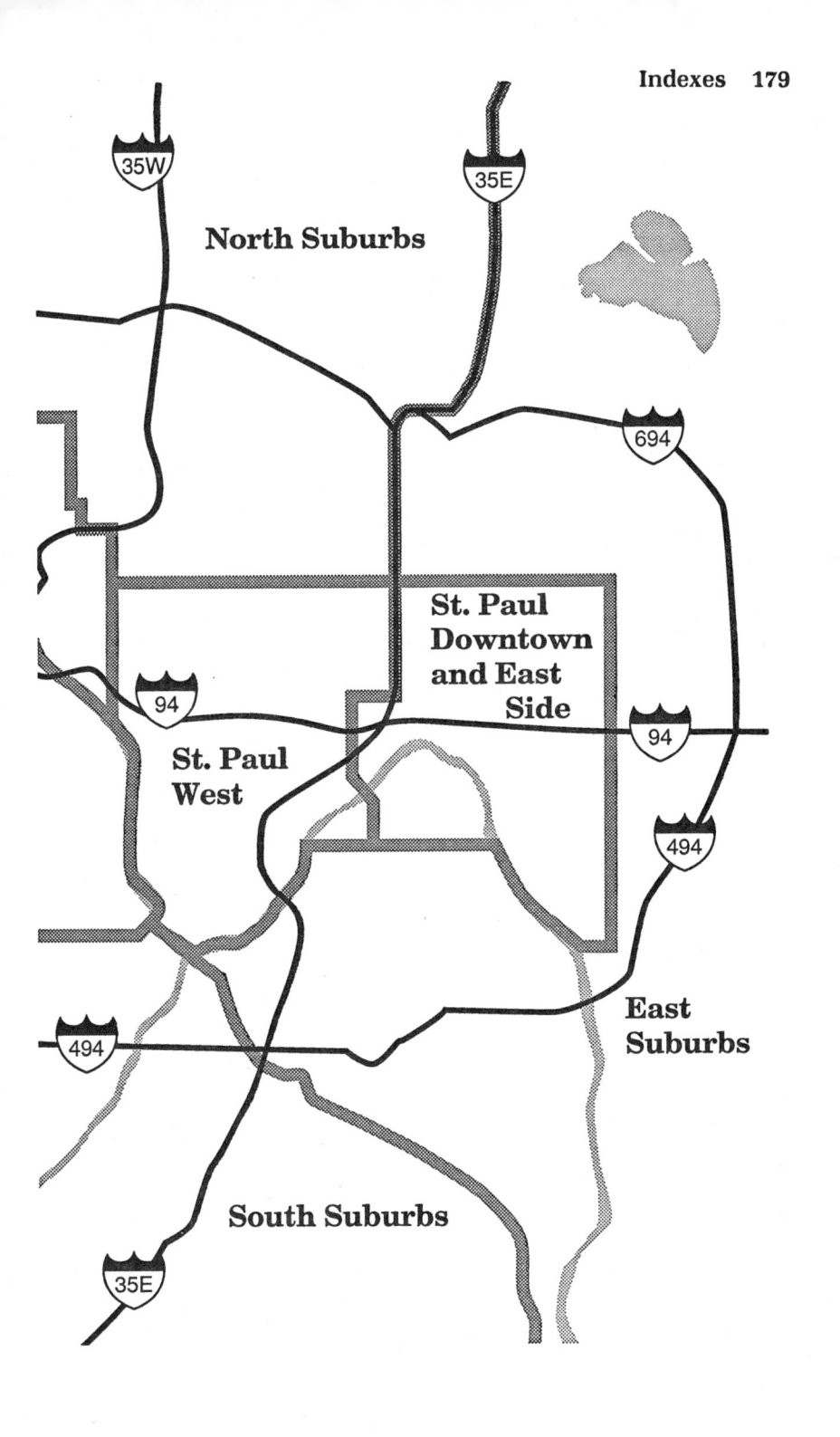

**North Suburbs**

**St. Paul Downtown and East Side**

**St. Paul West**

**East Suburbs**

**South Suburbs**

# ALPHABETICAL INDEX

Acapulco Bar & Grill ................ 7
Acropol Inn ............................. 8
Afghan, Da ............................ 30
Afton House Inn ..................... 9
Alfaro's Mexican
  Restaurant ........................ 123
Al's Breakfast ...................... 123
Amenacer, El ....................... 131
Annie's Parlour .................... 123
Anthony's Wharf ................... 10
Austin's Steak House ........... 11
Azur ....................................... 12
Barbary Fig ........................... 13
Bayon .................................. 124
Beijing ................................... 14
Bigsby's Cafe ...................... 124
Black Forest Inn ................... 15
Blue Mountain Coffee
  House ............................... 124
Blue Nile ............................. 124
Blue Point ............................. 16
Bocce .................................... 17
Brit's Pub & Eating
  Establishment ................... 18
Broder's Italian Cucina ....... 125
Cactus Willie's .................... 125
Cafe Brenda ......................... 19
Cafe di Napoli ...................... 20
Cafe Latte ........................... 125
Cafe Metro .......................... 126
Cafe Royale, Le .................... 65
Cairo Cafe .......................... 126
Caravan Serai ...................... 21
Caravelle ............................ 126
Caribbean, Harry Singh's ..... 49
Carrousel, Le ........................ 66
Caspian Bistro .................... 127
Cecil's Delicatessen ............ 127
Chez Bananas ...................... 22
Chez Colette ......................... 23
Chez Daniel .......................... 24
Chez Paul ............................. 25
Christos ................................ 26

Ciatti's .................................. 27
Cindybad Bakery & Deli ...... 127
Cityscape Deli .................... 128
Coco Lezzone ....................... 28
Cognac McCarthy's ............. 128
Corby's on the Croix ............ 29
Coronado Foods .................. 128
Corvina, La .......................... 62
Cossetta's ........................... 129
Creamery ............................ 129
Cucaracha, La .................... 138
Da Afghan ............................ 30
Dakota Bar & Grill ............... 31
D'Amico Cucina ................... 32
Deco Restaurant ................. 129
Delites of India .................... 33
DiMaggio's Sports Bar,
  Pizzeria & Grill ................ 136
Dixie's Bar & Smokehouse
  Grill ................................... 34
Dock Cafe ........................... 130
Dover Restaurant & Bar ....... 35
Duggan's .............................. 36
Dunn Brothers Coffee ......... 130
Dupsy's African Cuisine ..... 130
Edwardo's Natural Pizza .... 131
El Amenacer ....................... 131
El Meson ............................ 131
Emily's Lebanese Deli ........ 132
Emporium of Jazz ................ 37
Faegre's .............................. 132
Fair Oaks Hotel &
  Restaurant ......................... 38
Far East ............................... 39
Farmington Steak House ... 132
Figlio .................................... 40
Fitzgerald's .......................... 41
510 Restaurant .................... 42
Forepaugh's ......................... 43
Gallery 8 ............................. 133
Gasthaus Bavarian Hunter .. 133
Gasthof zur Gemutlichkeit .. 133
Gingham Kitchen Cafe ....... 134

# Alphabetical index (continued)

| | |
|---|---|
| Giorgio's ................................. 44 | Le Peep .................................. 139 |
| Good Earth ........................... 45 | Lexington .............................. 67 |
| Goodfellow's .......................... 46 | Living Room ......................... 68 |
| Green Mill ............................. 134 | Loon Cafe .............................. 139 |
| Gustino's ............................... 47 | Loretta's Tea Room ............. 139 |
| Harbor View Cafe .................. 48 | Loring Cafe ........................... 69 |
| Harry Singh's Caribbean ....... 49 | Lotus ...................................... 140 |
| Heartthrob Cafe ..................... 50 | Lowell Inn ............................. 70 |
| Holy Land Bakery & Deli ..... 134 | Lowry's .................................. 71 |
| House of Breakfast Plus ....... 135 | Lucia's ................................... 72 |
| Hoyt's, J.D. ............................ 54 | Lufrano's ............................... 140 |
| Ichiban .................................. 51 | Lundi's Pastry ...................... 140 |
| It's Greek to Me .................... 135 | Mai Village ............................ 141 |
| Jacob's 101 Lounge ................ 52 | Mama D's ............................... 73 |
| Jax .......................................... 53 | Mama Mia's ........................... 74 |
| J.D. Hoyt's ............................. 54 | Mancini's ............................... 75 |
| Jenning's Red Coach Inn ....... 55 | Manny's Steakhouse ............. 76 |
| Jerusalem's ........................... 135 | Market Bar-B-Que ................ 141 |
| Jien Fung .............................. 56 | Marquette Cafe ..................... 141 |
| Joe DiMaggio's Sports Bar, Pizzeria & Grill ................. 136 | Meadows ................................ 142 |
| Joe Senser's Sports Grill & Bar ..................................... 57 | Meson, El ............................... 131 |
| | Milano's ................................. 142 |
| Jose's American Grill ............ 58 | Minnesota Zephyr ................. 77 |
| Juanita's ................................ 136 | Mirror of Korea ..................... 78 |
| Keefer Court .......................... 59 | Mud Pie .................................. 142 |
| Keys ....................................... 136 | Muffuletta in the Park .......... 79 |
| Khan's Mongolian Barbecue ........................... 137 | Murray's Restaurant & Lounge ............................... 80 |
| Khyber Pass .......................... 60 | My Le Hoa ............................. 81 |
| Kikugawa ............................... 137 | Nankin ................................... 82 |
| Kincaid's Steak, Chop & Fish House ................................ 61 | New French Cafe .................. 83 |
| | New Riverside Cafe .............. 143 |
| Kramarczuk's Eastern European Deli .................. 137 | Newport SeaGrill ................... 84 |
| | Nicollet Island Inn ................ 85 |
| La Corvina ............................ 62 | Nikki's .................................... 86 |
| La Cucaracha ....................... 138 | 19th Hole, Ted Cook's .......... 155 |
| Lan Xang .............................. 63 | Nora's .................................... 143 |
| Latour .................................... 64 | No Wake Cafe ....................... 143 |
| Le Cafe Royale ...................... 65 | Nye's Polonaise Room .......... 87 |
| Le Carrousel ......................... 66 | Odaa ...................................... 88 |
| Leeann Chin ......................... 138 | Old City Cafe ........................ 144 |
| Lee Nue Village .................... 138 | Old Country Buffet .............. 144 |
| | Origami ................................. 89 |

# Alphabetical index (continued)

Pacific Club............................144
Pasqual's Southwestern Deli.................................145
Peep, Le................................139
Peter's Grill...........................145
Pham's Vietnamese Cuisine 145
Pickled Parrot..........................90
Polo Italia..............................91
Poodle Club............................146
Popeye's Famous Fried Chicken.............................146
Porky's.................................146
Porter's Bar & Grill..................147
Poulet..................................147
Pronto Ristorante.....................92
Quail on the Hill......................93
Quang Pastry & Deli................147
Rainbow Chinese Restaurant 94
Red Sea................................148
Rick's Ol' Time Cafe................148
Ristorante Luci........................95
Rosewood Room....................148
Rossini's Trattoria....................96
Royal Orchid..........................97
Ruam Mit Thai.......................98
Ruby's Cafe..........................149
Rudolph's Bar-B-Que.............149
Russian Piroshki & Tea House.................................149
Russian Village......................150
Sahari..................................150
St. Martin's Table...................150
St. Paul Grill..........................99
Sakura................................100
Samurai Steak House.............101
Sasha's Deli & Grill................151
Sawatdee............................102
Scandia Bakery & Konditori............................151
Scott Kee's Tour de France.115

Scully's................................103
Senser's Sports Grill & Bar, Joe......................................57
700 Express..........................151
Seward Community Cafe.....152
Sherlock's Home....................104
Shilla Stone BBQ..................105
Shuang Cheng......................106
Sidney's Pizza Cafe...............107
Signature Cafe......................152
SkyRoom.............................152
Smoke House.......................153
Sri Lanka Curry House.........153
Studio Restaurant.................153
Suzette's Cafe Exceptionale 108
Suzume...............................154
Swiss Alps...........................109
Szechuan Express.................154
Table of Contents.................110
Taj Mahal Groceries & Restaurant...........................154
Tandoor Restaurant..............155
Tay Do.................................111
Ted Cook's 19th Hole...........155
Tejas...................................112
Thanh Quan........................155
Times Bar & Cafe.................113
To Chau..............................114
Toulouse.............................156
Tour de France.....................115
Trieu Chau Village...............156
Trout-Air Restaurant............156
Trung Nam French Bakery.157
Tulips.................................116
Two Pesos..........................117
Village Wok.........................118
Wienery..............................157
Windows on Minnesota.......119
Yangtze..............................157
Yvette................................120

# Order form

If **Jeremy Iggers' Twin Cities Restaurant Guide** is unavailable at your local bookseller, you can order copies direct from the publisher. Single copies are $9.95 each; Minnesota residents must add 6½% sales tax, for a total of $10.60. We will pay for shipping and handling. Just return this form with your check, made payable to Beyond Words. (Please do not send cash.) You should allow two to four weeks for delivery.

☐ Please send me ☐ one copy / ☐ two copies of **Jeremy Iggers' Twin Cities Restaurant Guide** for $9.95 each, plus tax where applicable. Enclosed is my check for _____ .

**SAVE** by ordering three or more copies.
☐ Please send me _____ copies of **Jeremy Iggers' Twin Cities Restaurant Guide** for **$8.95** each, plus tax where applicable. Enclosed is my check for _____ .

Name: _____

Address: _____

City: _____

State: _____ Zip: _____

Please return this form with your check to:

**Beyond Words Editing & Publishing**
P.O. Box 130576
St. Paul, Minnesota
55113-9998